After Awareness
My Journey Through Betrayal

Written by:
Kimberley Fisher, Ph.D.

And the day came when the risk to remain tight in a bud was more painful than the risk it took to blossom

~ Anaïs Nin

DEDICATION

To my children, Karter, Mona, Karson, Kaiden, and Kylie. My greatest gifts!

ACKNOWLEDGEMENTS

My editor, Cat Margulis (catmargulis.com)—thank you for your brilliance. Your support and encouragement have been a true gift, and I am filled with gratitude that our paths crossed.

My friends and family—thank you for always being there to love and support me throughout this journey. You know who you are and the significance you hold in my life.

My husband, Geno—my everything. Words of gratitude cannot fully express my feelings for all that you have brought into my life. I am especially grateful for the time and space you offered me since my retirement, which allowed me to finish this book. I am forever yours.

CONTENTS

INTRODUCTION 7

LESSON ONE
Awareness allows truth to be revealed 9

LESSON TWO
You can teach only what you have been taught 37

LESSON THREE
Trust your gut instincts as inner wisdom 72

LESSON FOUR
Often, lessons learned in childhood must be unlearned in adulthood 97

LESSON FIVE
Choosing your own life script requires courage 128

LESSON SIX
Learn to forgive imperfect parenting 165

LESSON SEVEN
Addiction is an opportunity for change 186

LESSON EIGHT
Our children will teach us, if we let them 222

LESSON NINE
Relationships are a mirror for one's own true self 248

LESSON TEN
Life is a precious gift 269

EPILOGUE
Letter to My Children 299

Introduction

*"There is no greater agony
than bearing an untold story inside you"*

~ Maya Angelou

Throughout my life I have always found solace in the presence of a higher being. I call this presence God. To me, God represents the life energy that envelopes and connects each of us to our mother earth and to each other. As my life has unfolded, I have come to recognize that my purpose on this earth is to learn the lessons that I need to learn in order to achieve my own self-healing. My life lessons have offered me the gift of awareness and through this gift I have found myself.

In the following pages I share ten life lessons that I have learned as I walked through the many different phases of my life. Each lesson was possible thanks to an awareness that life events help create opportunity for each of us to learn a lesson or heal a wound. These opportunities allow us to become the person that we are meant to be. For me, my lessons were the culmination of an intense desire to heal the wounds from my childhood so that I could become the mother that my children deserved me to be. I, innately, understood that I had not been parented by healthy parents who could mirror the kind of parent that I wanted to become. Instead, I grew up in a family that was immersed in secrets. To this day there are many details about my life's history that remain unknown. This reality makes the truth very important to me. I have witnessed how secrets can negatively impact family dynamics and create distance between relatives. It's why I was always driven to seek the truth for myself. I firmly believed that healing my childhood wounds could and would occur through knowing the truth. This desire to seek help beyond what I had been taught led me to many life teachers, coaches, therapists, and friends who have loved and supported me on my journey. I share my story with the hope that it can serve as a light on the path for others seeking their own truth, awareness, and healing.

While all the stories in this book are based on real experiences, some names and identifying details have been changed to protect the privacy of the people involved.

LESSON ONE

Awareness allows truth to be revealed

Awareness is our ultimate state of "knowing." It is the intangible means of understanding our connection to the universe and to each other. This was not something that was taught to me, instead it was something that I came to recognize after I left my childhood home and moved out into the open world. I was raised in a small town with little access to the world outside, which limited my understanding of everything. So, when awareness, also known as consciousness or truth, began to reveal itself to me, I was hesitant to understand or even recognize what was being unmasked before me. It was like a gut feeling that one has when they do not yet possess the wisdom of understanding. This was my state of being for many years. Recognizing these opportunities for awareness finally came through trusting myself over and over again. I believe that we are all born with an innate understanding of both ourselves and our world around us, but unfortunately, we often lose this connection in childhood through our own life experiences. Being able to connect to ourselves and to the world around us is the gift of awareness.

Awareness comes, usually not be choice or approval, but often through trials and tribulations. It arrives over and over again, louder and louder, gaining volume and momentum one step at a time until it is identified and received. For me, awareness came slowly, allowing me the time I needed to be able to recognize when it arrived.

I started writing this book in the winter of 2000. At that time, I was finishing my doctorate degree, unemployed, financially vulnerable and for the first time in 22 years, I was alone on Christmas. My divorce from my husband, Jay, had recently finalized, after more than three years in the legal system, and my children were spending the holidays with their father. Despite these circumstances, I remember having immense feelings of thankfulness. The previous three and a half years of my life had finally brought me to a place of contentment. I was grateful for the gift of awareness that was beginning to be revealed to me and for the first time in my life, I knew that I was not on this journey alone. Just knowing that God was with me was a comfort that transformed all the lessons that I had learned and had yet to learn.

Awareness startled me awake on November 30, 1995, and there was no missing the arrival. It was eight days after my youngest daughter's first birthday. I had been married to my husband for 17 years. We had four beautiful children together and had completed our family with the addition of our oldest daughter, Mona, who came to live with us when she was a young teenager. At that time, my life consisted of going to college to finish my PhD, raising my five children, and working part-time as a lactation consultant. I was doing life, as I knew it. What I did not know was that my husband had a completely separate life from ours together. His secret, when revealed, would rip our family apart, but it would also allow me the opportunity to build a spiritual relationship with God that would sustain me through the many life lessons that lay ahead of me, which were, at times, hell on earth.

In November of 1995, I was living in a small town in Western North Carolina and commuting to the University of Virginia (UVA) in Charlottesville, Virginia, for my doctorate degree in nursing. The commute was, for me, a mere 600 miles round trip. There were times, while making this weekly trip to

Virginia, often with my infant daughter in tow, that I questioned if my long commute was something out of the ordinary. I had accepted that getting an advanced education was worth any sacrifice that I had to make, but as time passed it became harder for me to justify my experiences. Then, when the dean of my doctoral program informed me that I was commuting the furthest of any other doctoral student they had **ever** had in my program, I recognized, with clarity, the reality of my situation. Confirmation continued, as I met more students and faculty, each appearing shocked when I revealed to them the details of my weekly commute. Having my infant daughter join me in my second year, as I made these weekly travels, compounded an already difficult, and often, challenging situation.

My schedule for each semester differed depending on the classes that I was taking. Prior to the birth of my daughter in 1994, I was living in a small mountain community in southern West Virginia. I had started working on my doctorate degree in the fall of 1993. Initially, I would leave my home early in the morning on Mondays in order to arrive at UVA in time for my first class of the week. I was usually able to combine my classes so that all of them were scheduled from Monday through Wednesday. My husband, Jay, and I had a private pediatric practice where we provided primary care for children. My husband was a practicing pediatrician, and I was a nurse practitioner. Leaving for school early on Monday mornings meant that I could be home longer to ensure coverage for our private practice. Otherwise, while I was gone, Jay would have to cover both our private practice as well as his busy hospital practice. He worked parttime in our primary care clinic and full time at the hospital, which meant that I would typically cover the private practice twenty-four hours a day, seven days a week, while he covered his hospital practice. At that time, my commute from West Virginia to Virginia was 210 miles, which took approximately three and a half hours of driving time.

By the time we moved to North Carolina in 1994, my commute was extended to 278 miles, with a driving time of four and a half hours. There were a few semesters, over the first two years, when I had to stay at UVA from Monday through Thursday. However, after my daughter was born, I limited my classes to three days, since it meant my having to take her with me so that I could continue to breastfeed. I had enrolled my daughter in a daycare that was located close to the university. I purchased a pager, which the daycare used to contact me in case of any emergency. The pager was out of necessity since I was commuting a long distance, and there was no one else who could be listed as my secondary contact. Since starting school in 1993, I had been staying in the same hotel located in downtown Charlottesville. The staff at the hotel became a source of support for me and subsequently for my daughter, during our weekly visits to Virginia. This was my life for three to four days every week from 1993 through 1995.

As my daughter got older, she wanted more stimulation than her overworked mom could provide her in a hotel room, so, at night we would often ride the elevator up and down so that she could look out over the atrium of the hotel as we let people on and off our elevator. I would sit in the corner of the elevator, with my notebook and pen, working on my school assignments, while my daughter remained fascinated by the ride up and down. This was often our nightly routine after she got too old to be contained in our small hotel room!

When my daughter was a little over 12 months of age, I stopped taking her with me. When she was no longer making the weekly trip with me, I brought my electric breast pump instead. To maintain my milk supply, I had to adhere to a strict three-hour pumping schedule. This meant I had to pump in my car as I drove to and from Virginia, since I usually arrived in time to start my first class of the week. I would plug in my adapter and carefully position both bottles with one arm while I drove with the other hand. I often thought about the possibility of being stopped by the police, since driving the speed limit was not necessarily something that I always maintained. It was 1995, long before all the current advances in pumping gear for lactating mothers.

While I was away at school, my mother stayed at home with my older children, since Jay was often busy with his work. My mom traveled from West Virginia to North Carolina each week to watch our children for three to four days a week. This was our life in 1995. Jay had moved us, yet again, to a new city so that he could find the "perfect" place to practice medicine. The problem was that there was no perfect place, because everywhere he went, he took his SECRET with him. As his wife, friend, and lover, I knew nothing about his secret. However, what I did recognize was that Jay was having a hard time finding that perfect place.

Starting back in 1986, we had moved our little family to Mississippi from Kentucky, where Jay had completed both his residency (mandatory, post-graduate training to gain specialty experience in the chosen field of study) and fellowship (advanced subspecialty training completed after residency) after medical school. Jay explained to me that he had found his perfect job in Mississippi. After six years in Mississippi, he decided he found his new perfect job in our home state of West Virginia, so, in 1992 we moved again. This time we moved to the mountains of West Virginia. However, just three weeks after we had moved, Jay was already trying to find yet another "perfect" place to move. In 1993, while still living in West Virginia, I started my doctoral training at the University of Virginia and I had assumed that our next move would take us closer to my school and, thus, enable me to finish my degree. While this was my assumption, it never really occurred to me that we would be moving again so quickly! However, just two years after having moved to West Virginia, Jay decided to move us to a small town in North Carolina, which extended my drive to school even further. Initially, when Jay first told me that he wanted us to move to North Carolina, I refused to go. I was adamant that I was unwilling to move again! I was at that time, a few months pregnant with our youngest daughter and I was keenly aware that moving to North Carolina would extend my already long commute to school. After Jay's persistent persuasion, which involved discussing potential scenarios about the safety of our unborn daughter in a town lacking high-risk pregnancy or neonatal specialists, I ultimately gave in to the pressure and agreed to the move.

After moving to North Carolina and having my commute extended, there were many days that I questioned whether or not I would really ever be able to complete my PhD. Having a longer commute not only extended my drive to and from school but it also made it more difficult for me to be present for the many school events that my older children were involved in during that time. Even though I liked the UVA program that I was in, I made the decision to try and change to the UNC-Chapel Hill doctorate program, so that I would have a shorter commute. Unfortunately, I quickly discovered that transferring to a new program would mean that I would have had to start all over, as the philosophies of each program did not facilitate transferring students. So, reluctantly, I decided that since I was two years into my current UVA program, I would just finish where I was, even if it meant enduring an almost 600 miles round trip with either an infant or a breast pump in tow.

By November 1995, I was doing it. I was completing work for my PhD, working every weekend and taking care of my children, including nursing my youngest. The reason that I was able to do all of this was because I too, had a secret. I was using my eating disorder to control all the feelings of resentment, powerlessness, anger, frustration, and fear that I was feeling. My eating disorder helped me deal with the many feelings of worthlessness that I had felt throughout my entire life. Even with my PhD underway, I had convinced myself that I had been accepted into my current doctoral program because of some administrative error and not based on my own merit as a viable candidate for the program. I was terrified that this error would be rectified before I had time to complete the program. Despite maintaining a grade point average (GPA) of 4.0 throughout my program, I was convinced that I was in no way smart enough to get a PhD.

On Thursday November 30, 1995, I got home from school about 9:30 pm. My oldest son, Karter, who was 14 at the time, was home babysitting the other children. Jay was on call that night and he had been previously paged to the hospital. My mother had not come that week because Jay felt that he could watch the kids by himself, with Karter's help. When I arrived, I walked through the house and made my way into the kitchen, greeting all of my kids along the way. I then sat down at the desk in the kitchen and as my baby girl came over to me, I lifted her to my lap. While she nursed, I continued to chat with my older children as I went through the mail that had come during the previous three days that I had been away at school. There was an envelope addressed with my first initial "K" and my husband's last name. Ordinarily, I would throw away all the mail that was addressed to me using my husband's last name, since we did not share the same last name. I assumed that people who knew me would know that I had my own last name and people who were trying to solicit me because of my husband were not worth my time. The fact that I did not have my husband's last name was not because I was brought up believing that women have a right to keep their name if they choose, but rather, it was due to the hand of God paving the way for a time when I would need the strength of my own name to sustain me.

Jay and I had married in 1978 and at that time, I took his last name as my own. I gave up my own name as if I had no choice. The truth was I didn't know that I had a choice. However, after we had been married a few years, I decided that I wanted to have my own identity. The motivation for the many changes that began to happen for me during this time were directly linked to the opportunity that I had to pursue higher education. So, after 11 years of marriage, while pregnant with our third son, I made the decision to use my maiden name hyphenated with my husband's name. My husband was supportive of me using my own name until I, also, asked that my name be given to our children, before the birth of our youngest son. Jay rarely told me no, even if he wanted to. So, at that time I moved forward and hired an attorney who helped me change our two oldest sons' last names. Then when our third son was born, we just wrote his new birth name on the birth certificate. I was so proud to have given my name to my sons. I remember that my oldest son had a hard time with the transition of a different last name which lengthened his last name substantially. At that time, he was only eight years old and he often complained about having a new last name that he had to spell correctly in school, but eventually he settled into his new identity. I remained so pleased with my decision. Slowly, I could feel that I was beginning to emerge into myself.

    A few years later, before beginning my doctorate degree, I decided to remove my husband's name from mine and use only my own last name, since all three of our sons had both of our last names at that time. This was a decision that I had thought about for a long time. My circle of awareness had continued to expand, and I realized that the traditional practice of a wife taking her husband's last name was not the only choice that I could make for myself and for my children. I wanted my children to recognize that I saw myself as important. I hoped that this would allow them to recognize their own self-worth. My continued exposure to higher education was the real impetus for so much change that happened to me during this time. I felt so honored to be able to not only go to college but to succeed, over and over again, degree after degree. I wanted my children to know that I worked hard because of them. I also wanted to teach them about the importance of getting a higher education. When I was growing up, I had never viewed college as an option for myself. I was not necessarily a good student and I definitely did not test well. The opportunity for me to go to college was a gift. Jay gave me this gift. He was the one who helped me recognize that college could be a reality for me. He helped me register for college and he showed me what I needed to do every step of the way. My first semester in college, he actually walked me to and from each class for the entire semester. I remain eternally grateful that he believed in me until I could learn to believe in myself.

Once I began to find my own strength, then I began to also find motivation in having my own identity. So, I hired another attorney to do the name change for me. Dropping my husband's name from mine did not prove to be as easy a process as simply adding my last name to his. The law understood my request only if I were getting a divorce, which at that time, I was not. I had to go to court and swear before a judge that I was not changing my name so I could hide illegal or illicit behavior with my husband's name. The procedure to change my name proved to be a lengthy and expensive process, but I persevered. I was so determined to take back my name and no matter what obstacle presented itself, I kept moving forward. There was no one who understood my desire to simply right a wrong. I just wanted to exercise a right that I did not know that I had in 1978, when Jay and I married.

I naively thought that everyone, including Jay, my mom and my sister would be proud of me for the courage I demonstrated when I decided to take back my name. At that time in my life, these people were my biggest supporters. Their opinions of me and of the decisions I was making were very important to me. As Jay and I were driving back from my courthouse appearance that day, I could tell that he was upset. I eventually asked, "What's wrong?" He quickly responded, with his eyebrows furrowed, "What do you think?" He bellowed, "I can't believe that you really went through with it. How do you think that makes me feel?"

At that time in my life, I still felt that I was indeed responsible for how Jay felt, and I remember feeling hurt and very disappointed in myself. No one in my family circle understood my desire to take back my name. Initially, even I did not understand my instinct to take back my name. That understanding did not come until later.

As hurt as I was about how Jay reacted to my newly found independence regarding my name change, my mother's reaction left me almost speechless. My mother's reaction, at first, was no response at all. Then one day, several weeks later, my mom was sitting in my van in our driveway, with my youngest child, while I went into the house to get something. I walked out of the house about that same time the mail carrier drove up to deliver our mail. He asked my mom if this was the "Fisher" residence. This sounded like an easy enough question, but I arrived at the van just in time to hear my mom apologize to the mail carrier for the fact that her daughter had confused him by having her own name. I really did not feel like the mail carrier was confused, but what I did feel like was that my mom was ashamed of the fact that I had taken back my name. This one incident was the catalyst for a new awareness that I had about how my mom really felt about me and, more importantly, how I felt about her.

As hard as it was for my mom to accept my name change, Jay's parents were equally as troubled by my decision. They told Jay that they always thought that I was jealous of his successes as a doctor. My sister never even acknowledged my name change, although she later hyphenated her maiden name to her husband's last name. The name change was a huge issue. I had a chip on my shoulder and I dared anyone to call me by my husband's name. I will admit that I was a little overly sensitive about it and it was a constant source of discourse in both my immediate and extended families. Still, I was slowly learning to trust my own instincts and decisions and I trusted this was the right decision for me.

With this history about my name, it is easy to see God's hand in making me aware of my husband's secret. The letter that I received on November 30, 1995, was addressed with my first initial and my husband's last name. The return address was simply three initials from somewhere in California. I opened the letter. It was a bill for thirty-six dollars and some odd cents. I had no idea what this invoice was about and I immediately looked for a phone number to call. It was after 10:00 p.m. in North Carolina but I picked up the phone and dialed, anyway. I explained to the man who answered my call that I had received a bill from his company and that I had no idea what it was regarding. The man on the other end of the phone seemed surprised to be receiving a call from a woman and he kept telling me that there must be some sort of mistake and that I should return the bill to the company. I continued to insist on knowing what kind of business I was calling and after much hesitation and resistance he finally said, "I'm sorry ma'am, but this is an adult phone service."

I froze. I had two young teenaged sons in my house, and I assumed that they had not used this service, but I asked them anyway. They both confirmed my instinct. My second thought was that my nieces had been over to visit a few weeks earlier and perhaps they had done it as a joke. I paused to catch my breath as a sudden state of knowing came over me, followed by a sense of calm. I looked at the bill more closely, our home telephone number was clearly listed, on the top right corner, and then I knew. This was one of those moments, where God simply picked me up and held me tight as I picked up the phone to page my husband, Jay. My husband called me back immediately, as he always did. Even though I had always handled the finances for our family, Jay had one credit card he kept for himself, and it was paid out of his business account. I had tried on countless occasions to get him to have the statement mailed to our home address, but he never did. He continued to insist on paying it out of his business account. At the top of this bill was a credit card number. While on the phone with Jay, I asked him for his credit card number. I lied to him about needing it, telling him that I wanted to order something from the Victoria's Secret catalog. With God holding me tightly, I read the number on the bill as Jay was giving me the number for his credit card over the telephone. The first eight numbers matched, but the last four were different.

Then I looked closer at the bill and noticed that the service was provided in July, and it was now November. After losing his billfold in August, Jay had been issued a new credit card. This bill must have been misplaced and when it reappeared and the company tried to run it through with the old credit card number, it did not go through, so they decided to put it in the mail. Then instead of addressing it to "J" they mistakenly put "K" and Jay had left it for me to open, not recognizing who it was for or who it was from. Whether or not I was ready to know, I now knew.

I told Jay on the phone about the bill that I had received. He went completely silent. I said, "You did this, didn't you?" He then said we would talk about it when he got home, and he promptly hung up. Jay had never hung up on me before. I felt like someone had just punched me in the stomach. Time seemed to slow down, and I was unaware of how much time passed from the time that Jay hung up on me to the time that he arrived home. When he did, I was in our bedroom when I heard him come into the house, acting as if nothing had happened. Jay was good at not showing emotion. I could hear him in the front room talking to our kids. It was not unusual for our kids to stay up late, even on a school night, if I was coming home late from Virginia. I was standing in the bedroom listening to Jay chatting with the kids and finally, after a few minutes had passed, I yelled for him to come into the bedroom. He left the children in the front room and made his way to the back of the house, to our bedroom. I stood very close to him and looked him straight in the eyes as I said again, "You did this, didn't you?" His initial response was, "Just once, to see what it was like." I didn't know much about sex addiction then, but one thing I was sure of, was that nobody made calls to an adult phone line service just once. Suddenly, all of the blank spaces in my memory where Jay's explanation for something that I had questioned him about became very clear to me. I started to understand the times when he appeared distant for extended periods without any explanation, the instances when he had to leave for a trip on short notice, and the moments when he became anxious in a restaurant and insisted, we leave for no obvious reason. I had always recognized that Jay was resistant to having deep meaningful conversations. He was awkward in crowds and very uncomfortable around his peers. Initially I assumed that he was a very shy person, but over the years I came to see that it was deeper than just being shy. I had grown up around addicts and I recognized their similar behavior, no matter what the drug of choice might be. From nicotine, to alcohol, to food, or to work, every addict has one thing in common – their addiction is the most important thing in their life. When you have something that is as important as an addiction then you want your addiction to remain a secret; when you have a secret it is impossible to be fully present for your family. This was the moment when I recognized that Jay was an addict. In that moment, 17 years of unexplained behaviors began to make sense to me when I viewed them through this new and different lens.

When I was looking into Jay's eyes, I saw something that I had never seen before. He looked like a terrified little boy who had been caught by his mother doing something awful. Knowing, intuitively that I was not alone I said, "Oh my God, you're addicted!" He could no longer deny it and we both started to cry. I was crying for the betrayal that I felt knowing that my husband would do such a horrible thing as use an adult phone line service. Jay cried for the relief of finally having part of his secret revealed. I knew almost nothing about sex addition but somehow in that moment of time, I had an awareness that surpassed my general understanding of the addiction.

My heart was broken. I felt physically sick. My sickness may have also been as a result of my eating disorder, which I continued to use as a coping mechanism. Over the next few weeks, the knowledge of Jay's use of an adult phone service grew until it had encompassed our entire marriage of 17 years! It turned out that it also included the use of pornography and chronic masturbation. Initially, I was stunned by his confessions. But slowly, every feeling that I had related to my own unworthiness, began to emerge inside of me. I somehow felt responsible for Jay's behavior. How could my husband use an adult phone service unless I was failing him as his wife? Clearly, I did not have a true understanding of sex addiction! A year later, Jay's father confirmed my initial fear of blaming myself, when he told the therapist leading our family therapy session during one of Jay's treatment experiences, that his son would not have done any of these things if his wife were performing her wifely duties. By the time his dad said this I was in a different state of awareness and in that very moment, I simply gathered my things and left that family meeting. At that time, we were at a treatment facility on the West Coast. I changed my plane ticket and flew back home in time to celebrate my youngest daughter's second birthday. Finding blame for something that seems unfathomable is a normal human response to pain. I later forgave Jay's dad at the same time that I forgave myself for initially having my own thoughts of blaming myself for Jay's addiction.

Jay's behavior, after I knew his secret, changed. He seemed to smile more, talk more, and interact with our kids more. He appeared to actually have more feelings. I, on the other hand, became depressed and I felt like if anyone knew what my husband was doing or had been doing, that I would die. I began to lose weight, which Jay always noticed. I was never very big, but Jay liked me bone thin. At that time, I still had two more weeks of school left that semester, including major papers that I had to finish. I was convinced that this would be the time when I would have to drop out of school. I felt that there was no way that I could clear my mind, even for a minute, to concentrate on completing a paper. Ironically, that particular semester I had been assigned to work with one of the senior faculty on her own research project. Her project focused on the extreme sexual practices of college students. It was a qualitative study, which meant that there were numerous recorded interviews with students detailing their sexual practices since arriving at college. In academics, there are basically two types of research methodologies that are used –quantitative and qualitative. Quantitative research focuses on numerical data and statistical analysis, while qualitative research delves into detailed descriptions and interpretations. I was directed to listen to the recorded interviews for this project, listening for common themes or categories and then record the findings so that the outcomes could later be analyzed. I can remember the irony of my situation, as I listened to hours and hours of individuals describing their own extreme sexual practices, while still trying to reconcile the many revelations that were being shared with me by my husband. In that moment, I felt that I was not going to be able to complete any assignment that had to do with extreme sexual practices, yet I did it. Looking back at that time, I can clearly see God's hand in my life because I did complete all my work and I continued to do well in school.

Classes ended for me that semester after my Tuesday night class. Ordinarily, I would stay over that night and drive the 300 miles the next morning. Instead, I had an overwhelming urge to go home. I truly believed that there was something more that Jay had to tell me. Jay's truth about all that he had done around his sex addiction oozed out of him very slowly. He would gently reveal more and more every day until one day I actually told him that I could not hear any more. Sometime later, during one of our couples' therapy sessions, Jay confessed to me that he was hoping that he could get help, recover, and never have to tell me all he had really done over the years.

Anyway, that Tuesday night I was on a mission. Even though I had initially told Jay that I could not hear any more about the things that he had done, I had changed my mind. Now that the semester had ended, I was going to make Jay tell me everything, once and for all. I felt that if I could just know everything, then I would somehow be able to process all the pain in time to return to school the following semester. Obviously, my way of processing the pain, hurt and grief of Jay's behavior was unrealistic. But I proceeded with my plan to know everything.

I planned to leave immediately after my Tuesday night class ended, so I asked my professor if it would be all right if I used my breast pump during class. I did not want to pump in the car on my way home since it was so late at night. Doctoral classes are very small and mostly informal. I would not normally have asked to use my breast pump during class, but I was determined to end the pain that I had been living with since finding out about Jay's addiction. The other students in my class were supportive of me, and often joked later as they talked about how I had once used my breast pump during class. None of them knew what was going on at my home and I was determined that they never would.

My life at school was so different than my life at home. No one knew my husband, but they knew that we did not share the same name. Part of Jay's addiction was that he needed to have external praise from his peers to make up for his own childhood wounds deep inside him. Consequently, not only did we move often, but we always moved to basically the same place, only in a different state. The town was always small, with no more than two hospitals in the community. Jay was usually the only physician in the area that provided his specialty service, which allowed for much external validation for his skills as a physician. The truth is that he was and still is a wonderful man, but his addiction had taken over and made him very unavailable to his family. Everywhere we went, there was someone who knew him or knew of him and all the great things that he had done. In actuality, he did do a lot of great things and he was and is an excellent physician.

As for his family, we often felt left out. Our oldest son, Karter, started acting out in violent rages when he was about six or seven years old. He had started with head banging behavior when he was about three years old. Jay would often promise our two oldest sons that he would play ball with them the following day and then he would be paged into the hospital during the night and leave me to tell the kids that their dad was gone and would not be able to play with them, like they had planned. More than anything, our sons loved playing baseball with their dad! This occurred over and over again. Eventually, Karter was tagged as the "problem" in our otherwise healthy family, and we actually sought psychiatric help for his behavior.

The problem was not Karter; it was just that Karter was the only one in our family brave enough to show any emotion. From the outside, Karter looked like the problem. For me, I was using the restricting of my food at that time to control any feelings that I was having that were the least bit negative, and Jay was just absent from the family altogether and using his addiction.

Jay's addiction was not just about sex; it was about doing anything he needed to do so that no one would see what he was really doing. I had responsibility in all this, too, because I went along with many of the choices that he was making. For instance, on that rare occasion when Jay would take time off from work, we would go on a vacation. We went to Disney World at least once every year. We went skiing once or twice a year, and we held season baseball tickets for the Cincinnati Reds even though we never lived in Cincinnati or even in Ohio. Our vacations often included my mom, my sister or both. My mom and my sister were a big part of our lives and the lives of our children. Jay was determined to keep me distracted from what he was doing by surrounding me with my family. Jay used my sister and my mom to distract me, and I went along with it because I thought he was just being nice by always including them on our trips. I remember one time, while we were still living in Mississippi, I asked Jay to take some time off of work and stay home with us, as a birthday present to me. I did not want to go on another vacation; I just wanted him to stay home with us as a family for the entire day. For that birthday I received a beautiful diamond tennis bracelet – Jay did not take any time off from work. Jay looked like the perfect man to my family and to me, and both my parents often told me that the best thing that I had ever done was marry Jay.

The stage was set. I drove home that Tuesday night like a woman on a mission! I called Jay to let him know that I was coming home that night. I got home around 1:30 in the morning and Jay met me at the door. I walked in and I told him that I wanted to know everything that I needed to know about what he had done. I was standing over by the television and Jay was sitting in the middle of the den on a stool. All of our children were in bed asleep. My mom, who had cared for my children while I was at school that week, was upstairs sleeping. I had my arms folded as I was trying to brace myself to hear whatever it was that he was going to tell me, or so I thought. Then he said it, the words that I had feared the most since I had become aware of his addiction. He said, "I have been with a prostitute." I fell to the floor crying. I thought at that moment that I would surely die from the pain in my heart.

Since, day after day, Jay's confessions about partaking in phone sex kept changing and expanding, I knew that I was not hearing all that there was to hear about the "one prostitute" story. As I pressed him for more information, one prostitute grew to two and then from two to 13. First, he said that he never had intercourse with them but that he only masturbated with them. Then he admitted to having intercourse with one. I could have killed him that night, but I was too broken to even look for a weapon. Instead, I got in my car and drove to the grocery store parking lot less than a mile from our house and I called my brother, Knox, on my car phone. I was screaming, "Knox, Knox!" I could not even say any words for a few moments; I just wanted to die. I told Knox what I knew. At that time, Knox was a successful therapist in Memphis, Tennessee, specializing in addiction. Knox calmed me down and told me what to do, step by step. First, I was to go home and tell Jay to leave the house. Then I was to go upstairs and wake our mom and tell her everything. Then, I was to call Knox back after all that was completed.

I went home and like a robot, I did everything that Knox told me to do. Jay left the house that night. I woke up my mom and asked her to come downstairs. My mom could tell that there was something wrong and the fact that it was almost three in the morning was the other clue that a crisis was occurring. Remembering that you can only give away that which you were given, and knowing that my mom was never given the love and attention she needed by her parents, set me up for what was to come to me from my mom. Still, I told her about Jay, anyway. She sat in the overstuffed chair in my den while I sat on the couch. I began to tell her all that I knew about what Jay had done and I included the phone sex as well as the prostitutes. My mom sat there, starring forward, never making eye contact with me. There were no words spoken for a long time. Then while still looking straight ahead, she said, "At least he doesn't drink." In that moment, I could feel that there would be nothing more to come from her as far as support and I told her to go back to bed. I lied to her and told her that I was also going to go to bed, as well. I called Knox and lied to him, as well, telling him that I was okay and that I would call him back in the morning. Then I paged Jay. Without a doubt, I was addicted to this man. I cried on the phone to Jay and I begged him to stop the pain in my heart, but he could not take away my pain. Even though I knew on an intellectual level that no one could remove the pain that had consumed me whole at that point, I still wanted so desperately to remain connected to Jay. Jay was my anchor. He was everything to me and I could not imagine my life without him in it.

    The knowing that I now had seemed to consume my whole being but still, somehow, I could feel God's presence all around me. Letting go of Jay and the dream of who I was with him would be a necessary step in my growth and evolution. What I would find at the end of that journey was myself. Awareness was slowly revealing the truth to me, about Jay and about myself, and in this moment of immense pain I began to take solace in finally knowing the truth. Somehow, I began to trust the process that was happening all around me.

LESSON TWO

You can teach only what you have been taught

When Jay and I married in August of 1978, I was convinced that we would grow old together. I was so in love with this man and I was confident that I had been blessed with the perfect husband after having survived my abusive first marriage to a man named Randy. Granted, I still had no concept of a healthy marriage or even of a relationship, but somehow, I believed this was it! Jay and I frequently discussed our common aspirations, which included diligently pursuing our careers, nurturing our children, and eventually traveling during retirement while engaging in mission work abroad. I believed in our dreams. More importantly, I believed in us. The awareness of Jay's addiction took so much from me, and the pain that was left often felt fatal. But I soon learned to never underestimate the power of God in my life.

One of the first things that I did, after the initial shock of finding out about Jay's secret, was to get myself together to try and make sense out of the crisis that I was facing. At that time, I truly believed that I had the power to heal Jay and I was convinced that I could somehow find a way to cure him and make him whole. But what I did not know was that I was actually on the path to my own self-healing. Time spent at school during the week, away from our home and away from Jay, gave me an opportunity to write, reflect and begin my own healing journey.

Ever since I first learned to write I have always found comfort in journaling. When I was younger, I had several small journals, with a lock and a key, and I would journal anything and everything that happened to me. Who I saw at school, who liked who, who was being invited to a party or was going to a movie – these events were all chronicled in my journals. I used to tape movie tickets and even pennies found on the ground during outings with my family and friends into my journals! My thoughts, feelings, and experiences were all captured in these treasure boxes of my thoughts. Journaling was my safe space; it was where I found solace. I continued to journal through my adolescence and into adulthood. When each of my children were conceived, I started a new journal for each of them. In their journals I recorded my pregnancy journey, their subsequent births and then chronicled significant events throughout their childhoods that each of them experienced. When our eldest daughter, Mona, became part of our family as a young teenager, I began to gather sentimental quotes that held special meaning for both of us. As each of my children turned 21 years old, I gave them their journal on their birthdays, so they could continue to document the rest of their own story. For my oldest daughter, Mona, I made her a photo journal filled with our family pictures and memories along with the special quotes that I had collected throughout our years together.

Journaling allowed me the opportunity to explore my feelings, thoughts, and fears. It also allowed me a safe space to explore the many issues that emerged within me, regarding my own childhood. Later, as I moved through my awareness and healing journey, I came to learn that you can only teach what you have been taught, and that made me realize how little I had actually learned as a child.

I was the third child born to my parents. My sister, Karla, was two years older, but she always seemed much older to me, as she would quickly become a mother figure to me and our younger brothers. Karla and I were both born in Durham, North Carolina. Our dad was a law student at Duke University. After my dad graduated from law school, he moved us to San Jose, California. Initially, I had no idea why my dad was drawn to California other than perhaps he wanted to be as far from West Virginia as possible, since that was where both sets of my grandparents lived. In 2023, my brother, Keith, and I went to visit my dad's only brother, Larry, in Virginia. During our visit I began to ask my Uncle Larry some questions about my dad. He told me that the reason my dad went to California after graduation was because he had failed the bar exam for the state of North Carolina, after getting drunk the night before the exam was scheduled. Apparently, my dad found out that he could practice law in the state of California without having successfully passed a state bar exam. So, off to California we went! I was only a few weeks old when we made the trip across the country from North Carolina to California. My dad was never comfortable staying in one place for very long and less than 3 years after we moved to California, my dad left our little family. I remember hearing my grandparents, on my mother's side, say that my dad had left with "someone." I'm not sure who this person was, but nonetheless, my mom found herself in California with three young children to care for. Eventually, my grandparents provided funding to my mom so that she could bring us all back to West Virginia. My dad's decision to leave our family and be with "someone else" would become the theme of our family throughout my early upbringing. This event was the first time that I have any memory of my dad leaving us, but this pattern of behavior would become the touchstone for our childhood.

During our time in California, I have very few memories of us as a family. I remember that it was hot and sunny. I remember playing outside in the yard with my sister, Karla, along with some of the other kids in our neighborhood. These memories are from a few of the pictures that my sister had of all of us playing in our yard during this time. Less than a year and a half after we moved to California my brother, Keith, was born. I recall Keith as an exceptionally large baby. Given my own small and frail stature as a child, he appeared to be quite a big baby in comparison. One day, he and I were both taking a nap together on a large bed. I remember there was a loud noise that woke me up and there seemed to be smoke coming out of the wall where the heating system was located. I tried to get Keith off the bed, but he was too big for me to lift. I remember having to roll him off the bed and then I started to drag him toward the door to get us both out of the room and to a safer place. I have no memory of either of my parents being present during this time, but I do remember that my sister was there and she quickly scooped up Keith and got us safely out of the room.

Another memory from our time in California, was being in the back seat of my dad's car and in the floorboard, below my feet, my dad had placed a box of puppies. My dad always had an affinity for dogs. He believed that he could make any breed better by selectively breeding dogs with certain traits, thereby refining pure bred dogs. His belief that he could refine any breed of dog was based entirely on the qualities that he perceived to be best. While we were living in California, his focus was on the Wire Fox Terrier breed. Our own terrier had had a litter of puppies and for whatever reason they were not up to my dad's standards. My dad drove me and the box of puppies to a large building and when we arrived, my dad took the box of puppies into the building, while I waited alone, in the backseat. He soon returned to the car without the box of puppies, and I never saw them again. Even as an almost three-year-old, I knew never to ask questions, so I never did. I always hoped that he had dropped them off at an animal shelter, but I have no idea what happened to those puppies.

Eventually, after my dad left us all in California, my mom was forced to get us back to West Virginia, where her parents and our other family members were located. I remember riding on the train from California to West Virginia. The train was very exciting to me as a little girl. Me and my sister and my little brother all had on matching outfits for our long train ride. I remember that they were red with white piping around the collar and along the hem of the skirts that my sister and I wore. I guess my grandparents must have sent outfits to our mom for our train trip back home. Appearance was always important in my family.

Even though my dad had abandoned his wife and three children in California, it remained important to my mom and grandparents that we "appeared" to be normal children traveling by train. I don't remember much about the train ride, but I do recall that my mom was holding my baby brother, Keith, on her lap as he napped. At one point, my mom fell asleep, and Keith started to slip from her lap toward the floor. I quickly got down from my seat and tried to push Keith up to mom's lap before he hit the floor. Unfortunately, this maneuver woke up both my mom and Keith and I was scolded for having gotten out of my seat. Ultimately, we made our way back to West Virginia. I am unsure of the timeline of when we arrived back in West Virginia or even when our dad returned to our family for one more attempt at being a dad! But sometime, soon, after our arrival, our dad was reunited with us in West Virginia. Once dad reentered our family, he moved us to a small town in West Virginia, called Vienna. Vienna was a few hours from where both sets of my grandparents lived and this would soon become the birthplace of my next brother, Kris. We lived in Vienna for a short period of time before moving to Parkersburg, a small neighboring town close to Vienna. Nonetheless, shortly after moving to Parkersburg, my dad left us, again.

During a recent visit in 2024 with my brother Keith, I asked if he had any childhood memories of our dad living in the house with us. He shared that he only had one memory of that time.

He then proceeded to tell me his memory of this event. He said that he remembered that he and dad were standing on the front porch of our house. He then said, "I don't remember where we were living at the time, but the porch was long and stretched across the entire front of the house. It was dark outside and me and dad were watching a large mother possum sitting on a low branch in the tree in our front yard and her back was covered with baby possums. The babies were all holding tightly onto the mother's back as she crawled across the low hanging branch in the dark." His mentioning of the possum triggered my own memory of this exact moment and I told him that I remembered the story as well. Keith continued with his story. "Suddenly the mother possum fell to the ground and all the little baby possums went scurrying across the yard. That's all I remember." I asked him if he remembered why the mother possum fell out of the tree and he said, "No, she must have just slipped off the branch." I responded, "No, she didn't fall out of the tree, dad shot her with a gun and killed her." Keith turned and looked at me in total disbelief. "Why would dad have a gun and why would he shoot her?" he asked. "I have no idea," I replied, as the memory played out vividly in my own mind. I was shocked when Keith relayed this story because it validated to me that it actually did happen. So much of my childhood is cloaked in darkness. Each of us kids lived in the same house together but our experiences of many of our childhood events differ. I never saw my dad hold a gun again and to my knowledge we never had a gun in any house that we lived. At the time of this event, we were living in Parkersburg, West Virginia. I was barely five years old, which meant that Keith was only three years old. I guess his three-year old mind could not comprehend that our dad would shoot and kill a mother possum, just because he wanted to. But that was our dad.

My dad dropped in and out of our lives during my early years of childhood. This pattern seemed to define our upbringing. He would appear, we would be a family for a brief amount of time, my mom would become pregnant and then he would be gone. This is how I remember my childhood. Later, when I was teenager, I began to understand that my dad was an alcoholic and a sex addict. It wasn't hard to figure out that he was addicted to alcohol. I can remember very few times when my dad did not either have a drink in his hand or, at least, smell of alcohol. My dad also married and divorced many times throughout his life. He was always looking for something or someone to make him feel good about himself. As a teenager, I did not know about sex addiction, but I did know that my dad had multiple affairs over and over again, despite having multiple marriages, which never seemed to last very long. My dad had a quick temper and could erupt into a rage at any moment. As children, we learned to keep our distance from him.

When I was seven years old, my dad left our family for the last time. At that time, we lived in a two-story house in a small town in southern West Virginia. The kitchen was small, even to me, as a young child. My mom was standing in the kitchen cooking and my dad was standing on the other side of the counter. My parents were arguing, and I could feel the tension in the room. My dad was about 6'4" and to a little girl he seemed like the biggest man on Earth. He smelled like alcohol, and to me, the smell of alcohol always meant trouble. In that moment, I remember that my dad looked down at me and told me that he was leaving. I immediately wrapped my arms around his leg and sat down on his foot to try and stop him from going. He quickly bent down, picked me up and placed me on top of our kitchen table and said, "Kimmie, your mom is making me leave!" He then turned and walked out the front door. I looked at my mom. She had tears in her eyes, but she did not say a word to me. I remember feeling angry at her for making him leave, but mostly, I was just scared of what it would mean for us as a family to have him leave us, again.

After Dad moved out, he would sometimes come back to our house when he was drunk. Our mom always cautioned us not to open the door when he arrived, but at times, it was impossible to prevent him from entering our home. I remember one specific time when he came to our house, and again, he smelled of alcohol. My sister, Karla, quickly put me and my two younger brothers safely into the upstairs bedroom closet. Karla had previously fixed up the upstairs closet, in the front bedroom, by placing a blanket on the floor where she had also placed some toys for us to play with. She also positioned a lamp inside the closet to take away the darkness. When my dad would come over to our house drunk, we would play in that closet, while my sister stood on the outside, periodically looking inside to make sure we were okay. On this particular occasion, I could hear my mom crying loudly in the bedroom next door, where her and my dad were "talking." In that moment, I was far too little to understand what was happening outside my safe closet, protected by my big sister. Nine months later my youngest brother, Knox, was born. By the time Knox was born, my dad had married someone else and had moved on to his new life with a new family. That night would be the last time he was at our house before he married his second wife.

    In 2025, I published a children's book, titled *This is Maggie's Story, Helping Children Understand Alcoholism.* The book was loosely based on this event from my childhood. Nestled into every illustration in the book there is a pink rose, which symbolizes awareness and truth for young Maggie as she struggles with her father's alcoholism, a secret long hidden by her family. In the book, Maggie learns to face the truth and the pink rose becomes a testament to the power of honesty, understanding, and the gifts that come when truth is spoken. This touching tale gently introduces children to complex family challenges, offering hope and resilience through Maggie's own journey.

I never thought of my childhood as hard or difficult. It was just my life and at that time it seemed perfectly normal to me. My mother's parents, my Grams and Gramp, worked hard to cover up the "tragedy" that was our life. They financially supported us throughout most of my childhood. At least I assumed that it was them that took care of us financially, although, this was never confirmed to me. After my dad married his second wife, he saw us only occasionally and was largely absent from our daily lives. Whenever he did make it to one of our scheduled weekend visits, he would stop by one of his favorite bars on the way to his new house in Huntington. He would sit each of us on a high stool at the bar and give us a coke and a candy bar in exchange for our silence.

We would stay there for as long as he wanted us to, primarily because we were all genuinely afraid of him. Additionally, soft drinks and candy bars were special treats that we usually didn't have access to in our daily lives. None of us ever told our mom that he took us by the bar every time he picked us up, until after we were all grown adults. As children we did not understand or even comprehend the dangers of driving under the influence of alcohol.

Once Dad was adequately intoxicated, he would drive us to his new family's house, where he lived with his new wife and her three children. His new wife had four children but her oldest son was no longer living in the home. This new wife was not really interested in adding more children to her already crowded home, but we came anyway. Eventually, my dad would legally adopt her three youngest children. Of course, this news came to us kids through my dad's mother, Grandmother Louise, as my parents were rarely forthcoming with such information. Other than our sparse visits with our dad, we spent very little time with his new family.

My dad and his new wife raised old English bulldogs and their house reeked with the odor of far too many dogs. My dad was obsessed with his dogs, and he seemed to love them more than any human in his life. He spent the rest of his adult life, wife after wife, obsessed with refining the breed of the Old English Bulldog. One of my children would later comment to me that he did not know that my dad was an attorney because he only knew him as someone who had too many bulldogs in his house.

Having a father who was an attorney, who had graduated from a prestigious law school, sounded like a grand start for any baby, but it was not so grand for me and my siblings. I was born into a family that was ruled by an alcoholic father and possessed by a co-dependent, depressed, somewhat narcissistic mother. I was raised in insanity. Even as a young child I recognized what others in my family seemed to overlook, which subsequently caused me to experience a lot of fear and anxiety. All I can remember is fear. Fear of my father's drunken rages. Fear of my mother's constant crying. Fear that we really were alone. Remembering again that you can only give to others that which you have received, I can see how this set the stage for my sister, Karla, to take care of our physical needs but not our emotional needs.

When I was around 10 years old, we learned that we had had an older brother, named Kenny, who died after living only a few days, and whom my parents were likely still grieving. The life and death of my brother, Kenny, was a secret in our family. My dad had arrived at our house in southern West Virginia one night and was, per usual, drunk. Being drunk was always accompanied with anger and soon after he arrived at our house my dad started yelling at our mom about something. He then blurted out, "You should tell them about their brother, Kenny!" My mom, paralyzed with despair and anger, responded to him with a look that scared us all. She shouted, "You promised you would never tell them about him!" None of us knew that we had an older brother who had died when he was just an infant. The details around his birth, life, death, and burial remained a mystery in our family, even after we knew about his existence. My sister later told me that she found his gravesite while visiting our grandmother Louise's grave, many years later. My sister and I have discussed this event a few times and we both believe that our parents had married because of an unplanned pregnancy with our oldest brother, Kenny. We believe that our mother kept his birth and death a secret because of her own shame of having become pregnant prior to marriage. The doctrine of our church had taught that pre-marital sex was a sin in the eyes of God and that sinners often suffered the rath of God. We know that this was a reality that our mom truly believed. The death of our brother caused a deep pain within our mom and even after it was revealed to us, she rarely ever mentioned him again. However, when she did, her despair was palpable to me. It seemed to be a grief that consumed her total being and this one event became something that she never really recovered from. No one in our family ever confirmed or denied the details of the narrative my sister and I created regarding Kenny's life, birth, and death, as none of the adults in our lives possessed the ability to tell us the whole truth. I was never sure if this was because they didn't know how to talk to us or if it was because they were just not interested in parenting us. Either way, this became a consistent behavior for all of the adults that surrounded us during our childhood.

    I know very little about my father's childhood. My father was the oldest of two sons born to my grandmother Louise. His younger brother was named Larry. Their biological father was not present in their lives. The details of my biological grandfather's life are not known to me. My father was raised by his mother and for some reason his brother, Larry, was raised by another family in the community. The family that raised my

Uncle Larry were considered to be an upper middle-class family. I was told that my uncle was raised by this family because he was good friends with one of their children, but, whatever the reason, my dad spent his teenage years alone, taking care of his mother. When my father was in high school, my grandmother Louise would often go out drinking late at night. Before my dad left for school each morning, he was tasked with first finding his mother, who was often in a drunken stupor, and then getting her cleaned up and tucked into bed. My grandmother Louise was a definitely a "girl who wanted to have fun." She married several times throughout her life, even though the exact number of marriages is not known to me. I do know of at least two step-grandfathers from my childhood. She was a fun grandmother to a child who was starving for attention. There was always tangible tension between my grandmother Louise and my dad. I knew from my dad that he believed that my grandmother had not been a nurturing, loving mother to him. In fact, my sister later found a poem that our dad had written about his mother when he was in high school. It is titled it "A Pitiful Mother" and he wrote it under the pseudonym, Eric Von Fishvich.

A Pitiful Mother

When thou are peacefully settled in bed,
A solid roof over head,
Open comes the door,
With a great sounding roar,
Thou Mother stagers in,
Thou can see she is soaked to the skin,
What flashes through thy mind,
Thou looketh and say, "can she be mine",
Who cares for me when sick,
When in need of clothes or such,
A silent prayer is said,
Wishing thou were dead
Rather than see thy mother this way,
And to hear her say,
Why art thou an unworthy son,
Who doesn't comfort me when work is done?
Thou canst neither reason nor sigh,
Because she is filled to the eye,
With alcoholic beverages and wines,
drunken when she dines,
But still, thou knoweth mother is the best
And hope that in heaven she will rest.

Obviously, my grandmother Louise had not provided her own children with the love and attention that they desperately wanted, needed, and deserved. However, she was a loving grandmother to us, as her grandchildren. Looking back, I wondered if my dad was jealous of how his mother would get down on the floor and play with us grandkids for hours. She would also pile us all in her car and take us to the drive-in to see a movie and buy us popcorn and candy. Whatever the reason for the tension between my dad and his mother, things never changed. My grandmother Louise died in her early 60s from a lifelong addiction to nicotine. Her relationship with my father remained unchanged. With the benefit of hindsight, I feel like my grandmother eventually recognized her shortcomings as a mother and tried to make amends by being a present grandmother to her grandchildren. However, this did little to heal the deep wounds that already existed between my father and his mother and between my father and his brother.

My Grams and Gramp, parents to my mother, were very vocal about how they felt about my dad. They did not hold him in high regard and they made their views known to all of us children. My dad was quite a character. He was a prominent lawyer, with a successful practice, drove a Buick convertible, while his ex-wife (my mom) and five biological children lived on the edge of poverty, with no car and little else. We never owned a car and to collect our weekly groceries we would all walk to the grocery store, each carrying home a bag of groceries. This ritual became increasingly embarrassing to us as we grew older and we would eventually convince our mom to let us walk to the grocery store at night, so that no one in our small town would see us walking home, carrying our groceries.

I was eight years old when my mother was put on total bed rest for almost the entire pregnancy with my youngest brother, Knox. My mom was so sick that my grandmother Louise hired a live-in housekeeper to watch over us. Her name was Irene and the only thing that I remember about her was that she was a terrible cook. Knowing that my dad had already remarried someone else, I often thought about what would happen to us if my mother died. I knew that my dad's new wife would not want us because she had four children of her own. My grandparents could not take all four of us, plus the new baby, because they were too old. I would often sit outside my mom's bedroom door and listen to her crying inside. I thought she was crying because she was so sick. I had no way of understanding how broken my mom was from the events that had happened to her during her life.

During times of acute distress in my young life, I often pretended to be someone else, a happier, safer self, and I named her Maggie. This was the name that I gave myself from my earliest memory as a little girl, and she is the inspiration for the character in my published children's book. I have no memory where the name Maggie originated from in my mind, but pretending to be Maggie comforted me in times of acute distress. I recognized from an early age that my family was full of names that started with the letter "K. I had five siblings in my own family whose names start with the letter K and I have four cousins whose names also start with the letter K. My dad's mother, grandmother Louise, had ten grandchildren and all their names started with the letter K. Even my dad's name, Kenneth, started with a K! It's the life script that I picked up from my family that led to me naming all of my children with the letter K, just as those before me had done. Maybe, that is why I chose a name like Maggie for my imaginary self. A name for a girl who came from a different family than mine. When things were happening in my life that were too much for me to understand or handle, I would pretend that my name was Maggie. Maggie lived in the same small rural community that I did, with one major difference: Maggie had two parents who loved and cared for her, and she was never scared. I started imagining my life through Maggie's eyes when I started elementary school. During my mom's pregnancy with Knox, I often pretended to be Maggie.

I thought my mom was sick. I did not understand that her heart was broken. My dad's mom, my grandmother Louise, took me and my three siblings to Virginia to visit our cousins (my dad's brother's children). We stayed with our cousins for most of that summer before my baby brother, Knox, was born. We arrived back home the day before school was scheduled to start. Knox was born the day after we got home. It was my first day of third grade. I was so relieved that he was born, but I was even more relieved that my mom had not died. After Knox's birth, my mom stayed home to care for him and she never worked outside the home until he started the first grade. Even though she was home for several years before Knox started to school, I still have more memories of my sister, Karla, caring for us, especially for Knox, than I do of our mom.

When Knox started the first grade, my mom began working as the financial secretary at our church. This was the first and only job that my mom had during my childhood. Karla was always responsible for us kids, typically taking our brothers home after school, while I would often wait at the church for my mom to finish work. Our church was located on our way home from school. I remember one day when I was sitting at my mom's desk at the church, waiting for her to be ready to go home. Our church had big metal trays where everyone's tithing was recorded, on a weekly basis. I often looked through the cards to see how much everyone was tithing to the church. One day I looked up my mom's card. Diagonally across the card in permanent black marker and underlined was written the word "<u>DIVORCED</u>." I felt so much shame about the fact that this was written across my family's card. I knew only one other person in my hometown with divorced parents, but her mom did not go to our church. I am sure that there were other children with divorced parents, but I was unaware of them and I was keenly aware that divorce was viewed by our church as a sin.

My mom was the token divorcee at the First Baptist Church. The rule at our house was that if the church doors were opened then we must be there, as a family. This church was all I knew of religion and spirituality. Unfortunately, this church's strict interpretation of the theological doctrine was encompassed within a very narrow belief of what was right and what was wrong. My church knew the answers to all the questions ever asked. Men were deacons, women taught Sunday School classes (a class held on Sunday mornings to teach children about religion) and abortion was the greatest sin. It was wrong to be divorced, but they made an exception for my mom on this one. White people were superior to black people. Being a homosexual was a choice and it was a choice that should never be chosen. You must be born again in order to receive God and go to heaven. This was all that I knew of the world as dictated by my little church on the corner of Poplar Street and 12th Street in a small southern town in West Virginia.

Anything that was said or done in this church, by those working in this church became my barometer for what was right and what was wrong. This was how I measured whether or not I was being a good person and a good Christian. The teachings of this church became the foundation for my life. What I learned at this church mattered to me. It is difficult to explain the importance of this church or measure the impact that it had on me as a child and even as the young adult that I would later become. This church became my extended family.

When I was in middle school, I had a Sunday School teacher who would make us kneel on our knees every Sunday morning, before we started our class, to check the hem length of our skirts. This was during the time of miniskirts. According to my teacher, the hem of the skirt must rest on the floor while on your knees. I always made sure that my skirt was long enough. The problem was not just that my teacher did this, but that I thought that all the teachers did this. I worried that my sister would be kicked out of the church because of the length of her skirt, which I knew would never come close to touching the floor. I never asked my sister, Karla, if her teachers measured the length of her skirts each Sunday morning, but I worried for that whole year until I got a new teacher the following year and found out that not all teachers measured the hem of your skirt before starting Sunday School class. At that time in my life, I did not feel like I had anyone to talk to about whether or not measuring the hem of one's skirt was not only done but what it would mean if your skirt was too short. Looking back, it is hard to imagine the profound impact those that worked in this church had on a child with a less than stable childhood.

My mom cooked the Wednesday night meals for our church. She was a wonderful cook. I would often hang around after the Wednesday evening service was over, while she cleaned the kitchen. I wandered throughout the entire church as if I owned it. I had been in every room of that church. The church janitor was named Henry, and he worked at that church for as long as I can remember. Henry and I were good buddies. He would often talk to me while I was waiting for my mom to walk home with me. Sometimes I would even help him clean. I thought of Henry as a nice old man. I learned the hard way that Henry was not a nice old man.

My sister, Karla, was fast becoming an expert seamstress. I remember a flowered, empire waisted dress that she made for me when I was in elementary school. It had a beautiful pink ribbon that tied in the back. The dress had a square cut neckline that was a little too big for my frail frame. One night while I was waiting at the church for my mom to get ready to go home, I went up to the fifth-grade classroom. I had gone up one flight of stairs when I met Henry coming down the same steps. He commented on my pretty dress. I was very proud any time Karla made me a new dress. Henry reached over and touched the ribbon on the front of my dress, and I remember feeling uneasy, but I stood still. Before I could react, he took his hand and slid it down the top of my dress and he touched my pre-pubescent breasts. I was paralyzed with fear. I never told anyone about what Henry did to me that day. For a while I was afraid to wear that dress again. One Sunday morning my mom told me to wear that same dress to church. So, I rolled up scotch tape and placed it along the square neckline so it would stick to my skin. From that day forward every time I wore that dress, I used the scotch tape. I was eleven years old. I learned to avoid Henry.

The Baptist church meant a lot to me throughout my childhood. As a teenager, we had a youth choir that allowed me the opportunity to travel and actually go on vacations. The times that I spent with the choir were some of the happiest times from my adolescence. Dan was our director and he was a true angel on this earth. He gave his time to all of us in the choir and he made each of us feel as though we were something special. We even once recorded a record in Nashville and every member in our church bought a copy of that record. I also know that Dan would leave cash in an envelope on my mother's desk at work, to help our family make ends meet. I had seen the envelope on my mom's desk many times and I recognized the handwriting of our choir director. He would leave it on her desk when he thought no one was looking but I always knew it was from him.

My entire childhood took place in the same small town, even though we often moved to different places in the same town, based on what was available to rent. I knew very little about our financial situation during my childhood. I never felt like we were poor because I believed that no matter what we needed, my grandparents would always provide for us. I believed with my "Maggie mind" that my grandparents were very wealthy. Both of my mother's parents had college degrees and worked as teachers for their entire careers, and to me, they were rich. I know that my mom tried to get my dad to pay child support on several occasions. I also know that he never paid consistently and the amount that he did pay still kept us near or below the poverty level.

In 2021, during one of my frequent trips to visit my sister, Karla, we stumbled into a conversation about our childhood. At that time my sister was providing around the clock care to our mom, who had Alzheimer's disease. We were talking about what it was like for us as teenagers and I told her that I never really knew much about our finances during that time. She told me since the age of 14, she had her "driving friends" take her to our dad's office, approximately 15 miles away, so that she could try and collect money from him to help our mom pay for our weekly groceries. She told me she would go into dad's office and talk loudly so that his clients in the waiting room would hear her. My dad had a very well-known law practice in Huntington, West Virginia. His image was important to him. It was even more important than providing adequate care to his ex-wife and his children. Karla used this as a way to extract money from him which, apparently, she did on a monthly basis. When she was telling me these stories, I was saddened to think that Karla had even less of a childhood than I experienced. I was also upset at our mother for allowing her 14-year-old daughter to take on the task of collecting the money that she was owed in the divorce agreement. My dad never paid his child support on time and my mother always told me when I questioned her as to why she did not get a lawyer to fight him for what she was owed, that there was no lawyer who would go up against my dad. I believed this excuse back when I was child, but now I see that my mom was completely depressed and unable to fight for herself or for her children – she left that to my sister, Karla. Over the years, Alhiezmer's disease slowly took our mother away from us. My sister provided around the clock care for our mother for many years, until her death in 2023. Karla never had children of her own; she mothered all of her siblings and in the end, she mothered our mother. I remain in awe of my sister Karla; we were all truly blessed to have her as our big sister.

My mom rarely went anywhere without all of us kids with her. Once, when I was in grade school, my mom mentioned that she was going out to play cards at someone's house, and I remember feeling so scared at the thought of her not being home with us. What if my dad came over? What if… this was a scenario that often consumed my thinking as a child. As she was getting ready to leave, I repeatedly told her that my stomach hurt. Despite my pleas, she continued her preparations and eventually departed when someone from our church arrived to pick her up. We had the phone number for the person she was playing cards with, and I called it several times, crying for her to come home because I felt sick to my stomach. She eventually came home. As I got older, I regretted how I treated her that night, but I had no ability to ease the fear that possessed me for most of my childhood. As time passed, it became harder and harder to think without my "Maggie mind" to help soothe me.

To my knowledge my mom never dated anyone throughout my entire childhood and adolescence. I never remembered her going out on a date and I did not even see that as strange. I would often hear people at my church whisper that no one would ever want to marry a woman who had five kids, but they were wrong. Eventually my mom did marry a man from our church. His name was Leonard. When I was going into my senior year of high school, my mom decided to start dating. Not only did she start dating, but she also decided to marry this man. The man that she was marrying was seen as a saint, according to the people at my church, for taking on a woman with so many children. I had never seen a saint before, but I was sure this man was not one.

Eventually, my mom told us that she was getting married and that we would be buying a house on the golf course. Granted it was a small nine-hole golf course that was being repurposed for a new sub-division, but regardless we were buying a house. We had never owned a house! I really didn't care who this man was. I was so impressed to not only be buying a house, but a house that I thought to be a mansion. I was going to have my very own bedroom for the first time in my life, in this new house! The news of my mother's wedding took all of us by surprise, but my sister, Karla, was absolutely blind-sided.

Karla had practically been our mother for as long as I can remember. She did all the cooking while our mom worked. She made dresses for herself and me and she even made suit jackets for our brothers for Easter. The news of our mom's impending marriage devastated Karla. I don't know what Karla was thinking but I do know that she was tormented by the prospects of having a man in our house. The night that we began packing to get ready for the upcoming move, Karla started screaming at me for some unknown reason. Karla was hot-tempered and that night she was especially quick to anger. At one point she picked up a portable radio and hit me on the head with it. By this time, we were both screaming loudly and as I fell onto the closet floor my mom came running into our bedroom and tried to stop Karla from hitting me. My mom grabbed Karla by the shoulders and tried to restrain her, but Karla bit my mom's thumb so hard that her fingernail eventually came off. My mom screamed and let go of her. Karla then jumped out of our one-story bedroom window. My memory around this time is foggy, but I remember that Karla was gone for a long time. In 2024, I asked Karla where she went during this time, and she told me that she went to live with our dad. She said that she was going to college at that time and that our dad's house was closer to her school, making her commute easier. When I asked her why she left that night, she said, "I was angry, as usual. I had taken care of mom and all of you and didn't need *him* (Leonard) to come into our lives." The impact of my mom's marriage had a profound effect on all of us, but it was especially difficult for my sister, Karla.

My sister was the only one of us who went to college right out of high school. I know that my dad paid some of her college tuition and I am not at all clear how long she lived with our dad after this incident. I did not see Karla again until right before my high school graduation when she stopped in front of our house one evening, while mom and I were sitting on the front steps. She did not get out of her car. Instead, she simply rolled down the window to ask mom about her immunization status related to the chicken pox virus. Apparently, Karla was being questioned about this by Marshall University, the college she was attending. Mom told her that she and I had both had chicken pox at the same time and that she should be immune. Karla thanked mom for the information and drove off. After this encounter, I started seeing Karla more often, as she slowly began to re-enter our lives.

After Karla left our home the night before we moved, our mom got married to Leonard. I was entering my senior year of high school in the late summer of 1973 when my mom got married, and we moved into the 'mansion' on the golf course. Suddenly, my life took a turn for the better. At least this was what my "Maggie mind" thought at the beginning of this new adventure. The man that my mom married was someone I did not know. He held beliefs about women, blacks and homosexuals that supported the doctrine of the Baptist church that we all attended. It was one thing to have those beliefs stated in the church, but it was entirely different to actually hear someone in your house state that a woman's place was in the kitchen. I did not hold my tongue very long with this man and we very quickly got into several heated battles over women's rights and the worth of a woman, in general.

Shortly after my mother married, I came to know that my continuing to live in our new house after my high school graduation was not feasible. I had no exit plan in place, but I just knew that, somehow, I was going to have to find a way to leave my mom's house. No one ever talked to me about my plans after high school. Neither my school nor my mom ever initiated a discussion with me about how to make plans for my future after graduation. I knew absolutely nothing about how to plan for my future and I did not feel that there was anyone in my life that could offer me any advice or support. My senior year of high school was spent living in a house that did not feel much like a home. I believed that the man whom my mom married had married her so that he could have someone take care of him. I heard from someone at my church that his first wife had died after a long battle with cancer. Apparently, this man needed someone to care for him and my mom fit the job description, perfectly. My mom was so busy taking care of her new husband that we were all forgotten. It was an especially sad time for my youngest brother, Knox. I was so self-absorbed in my own drama during this time, that I could not say that I even remember Knox during that time in our lives. I was focused on my own problems and on finding an exit strategy for leaving my mom's house.

After my mother re-married, she was as sad as I had ever seen her. She and her new husband went on a honeymoon after they were married and while she was gone, she ended up being admitted to the hospital. Her new husband, Leonard, took us to the hospital to visit her. I remember the first time that he drove us to the hospital. He was pulling into the parking lot and as he was slowly moving into his parking spot, he eased up close to the car in front of him and then quietly tapped it with his car and said, "That should do it!" He then put the car in park, and we got out of the car. This was my first indication that Leonard was not a safe driver. I would later find out that Leonard had very poor vision. Even though my relationship with Leonard was initially very strained, he later became a loving grandfather to my children. Until his death, he loved my children as if they were his own. I have very sweet memories of him holding Karson as a newborn, high on his shoulder as he rocked him to sleep, singing a Baptist hymn.

My mom stayed in the hospital for a couple of weeks and was subsequently released to come home. No one ever told us why she was hospitalized, but I suspect that she had some sort of mental breakdown. It was after this new marriage that she began to put on weight. She would often sit in the living room and eat in the dark. I had seen my grandfather have this same kind of relationship with food. Food, in my family, was a safe place to go when we felt anything, especially loneliness. Eating is an isolating addiction. I saw the way my mother and my grandfather used food when they thought that no one was watching.

Looking back, I can see that I was destined to marry an addict. I was not prepared mentally, socially, or spiritually to do anything else. Dysfunctional adults surrounded me for most of my life, and growing up, these were the only teachers that I had. They taught me all that I knew about adulthood. During my senior year, I had two marriage proposals. The question was, who should I marry? Is it any surprise, I made the wrong choice, with the information that I had? Just two months after my high school graduation, I fulfilled my life script and got married. I knew more than anything that I had to get out of my mother's house, and I thought the only way to do that was to get married. Up until shortly before my marriage, I was a virgin. I was the kind of virgin that did not even know about sexual intercourse until I was 17, and I was 18 at the time of my marriage. I remember how I found out about sex. My girlfriend, Terry, and I were sleeping in bed with my sister, Karla. I was sleeping in the middle. Someone that Terry and I knew, who was not married, got pregnant and we were discussing how this might even be possible. Karla got very frustrated with our childish conversation that night and she finally said, "Don't you know that he just sticks it in her!" Terry and I spent the whole night just waiting for morning to come so that we could discuss this new information on our morning walk to school. To say that we were shocked would be putting it mildly. We were shocked and horrified. We even thought that maybe Karla was playing a cruel joke on us! This was my source of information concerning sex, love, relationships, and marriage. Just a few short months after this conversation, I was married.

To say that I was naïve going into that marriage would be an understatement. I married a man that I didn't love to get out of my mother's house. I entered a relationship not knowing how or what to do, but I thought that was how marriage was done in my family. The truth is that I married my first husband, Randy, because I allowed him to have sex with me a few weeks before we married and I thought that meant I had to marry him. After all, sex before marriage was one of the cardinal sins that my church had listed in the "sin book." Throughout my childhood and adolescence, I was filled with self-loathing and low self-esteem. Prior to the proposal from my first husband, I had turned down a marriage proposal from someone that I knew really loved me because I felt that he deserved someone better than me. This set off a pattern of relationships where I would give up my power and diminish myself. It would be my life's journey to break that pattern.

I was so good at taking care of others, but I had a lot to learn about taking care of myself. I didn't have anyone to model this for me. When you first get away from the safety umbrella of your childhood home, it quickly becomes apparent whether or not the lessons that you learned or were exposed to in childhood have prepared you for adulthood. It did not take me long to notice the many deficiencies in my childhood education - academical, social, and even spiritual. Suddenly, I began to recognize that I didn't have many of the life skills necessary to succeed in life, that others take for granted. As each experience unfolded as I journeyed into young adulthood, I was reminded over and over again of what I had not learned in my childhood. Adulthood came anyway and eventually, I would be forced to learn those lessons myself that I had not already been taught in childhood. Including how to honor myself, so I could be a better role model for my children.

LESSON THREE

Trust your gut instincts as inner wisdom

Sacrificing myself for others is something that I learned well. I had watched expert teachers in my life sacrifice their own spirits in order to hold on to someone who did not want to stay. I watched my mom with my dad and then I watched my mom, again, give up her spirit to stay with her second husband. I watched my aunts with their husbands. I watched my grandfather with my grandmother. I watched my dad's many different wives try to make him stay but he never did. The adults in my life seemed to view marriage as a sentence to be served and not necessarily as a choice. By my senior year of high school, I had a "black belt" in caretaking and I was convinced I was ready for marriage.

During my junior year of high school, I dated a boy who really cared for me. His name was Dan. I dated him through the beginning of my senior year and then broke up with him when I became attracted to another boy named Randy. Randy would eventually become my first husband. Randy was one year older than I was and had already graduated by the time I was a senior. Randy and I dated on and off during the end of my senior year and I knew, at that time, that Randy was probably only dating me for one reason. It was common knowledge in our small high school that I was a virgin, and I had heard from some male friends, who took it upon themselves to protect me, that certain guys viewed me as a challenge. These same friends felt that both myself and my best friend, Terry, were very naïve and they took it upon themselves to screen anyone and everyone who had an interest in myself or Terry to ensure that their intentions were pure. These same friends had all expressed their many concerns to me about my dating Randy, but I was not deterred by their worries. After all, Randy was very attractive!

Randy was, at times, sexually aggressive with me, and for a long time I refused to have sex with him. After we had been dating for a few months, I did have sex with him in the backseat of his car. Afterwards, I was immediately convinced that I was pregnant. I assumed that if you had unprotected sex that you would get pregnant. My naïve thought process allowed for no other conclusion. For the next few days following that event, I was filled with guilt and consumed with fear about being pregnant and unmarried. Randy tried to reassure me that we should just wait and see if, indeed, I was pregnant, but I could not be consoled. Randy was taken aback by my response and eventually attempted to console me by proposing that we could get married if I were expecting. I'm uncertain whether he genuinely asked me to marry him or merely offered it as a remedy for my sadness, but either way, I said yes! As it turned out, I was not pregnant, but I did marry Randy in August of 1974, less than two months after graduating from high school.

Randy was my exit plan to move out of my mother's house. Not long before Randy and I had sex, my previous boyfriend, Dan, asked me to marry him. He was so very sweet, and I could see how nervous he was to even ask me, but I declined his offer. In that moment, I knew that Dan deserved someone who loved him as deeply as he loved me, and I did not share those same feelings for him. Earlier, during my senior year, Dan had given me an old English sheepdog puppy for my eighteenth birthday. After receiving this wonderful gift, I tried so hard to love Dan, but at that time I just wasn't capable of receiving or even understanding unconditional love from someone, so I broke up with him a few short weeks later.

As a young child, my mom had introduced me to old Doris Day movies from the 1960s. To me, Doris Day's life was like I imagined mine would be, in my "Maggie mind." In the movies, Doris Day had an old English sheepdog that caused all kinds of hilarious havoc, and I often imagined that my life would someday be like that of Doris Day's in the movie, *Please Don't Eat the Daisies* – where the biggest problem I would have to worry about would be what kind of mess had my sheepdog gotten himself into that day! I'm not certain if Dan bought the puppy to persuade me to marry him or if he simply knew how much I loved sheepdogs, but regardless, my dog Jeremiah became my loyal companion as I transitioned from my mom's house to my marriage with Randy. Soon, my life would look nothing like you'd see in a Doris Day movie.

I was still living at home with my family when I initially received my new puppy. I knew that my mom would not be happy with me having a dog in her house. I had chosen the name Jeremiah from the Bible, hoping that this would force my mom to like him, but to no avail. My mother did not allow any animals in the house, and Jeremiah was a large puppy who quickly became an even larger dog. I became quite creative in trying to care for him, while also attempting to appear to obey my mother by keeping him in the garage and never in the house. I would often sneak him into the house when my mom was either in bed or was not at home. One Sunday morning, as we all prepared to get ready to leave for church, I decided that it was too hot to leave Jeremiah in the garage while we were away. My mom and her new husband drove separately to church from the rest of us. After they had left for church that day, I put Jeremiah upstairs, in my brothers' bedroom, so that he would be in the air-conditioned house while we were at church. What I did not know was that my brother had opened the front window in his bedroom. Later that day we arrived home from church at the same time as my mom and her husband. As we pulled up to the house, we could see that there was something on the roof of our garage and as we got closer, we could all see that it was Jeremiah! He had gotten out of my brother's bedroom window and was now sitting on the roof of the garage. My mother was furious with me. She knew there was only one way that Jeremiah had gotten out of the garage and onto the roof. Suddenly, in that moment, my desire to leave her house intensified. I desperately needed an exit plan to leave my mom's house. Getting married would be my exit plan; I had no other options available to me. I started dating Randy soon after that event.

Randy and I had a big church wedding. My mother's sister, my aunt Jan, made all the dresses for my six bridesmaids and for the flower girl. The dresses were all fall colors of forest green, tan, and brown. They were long with a round scooped ruffled neckline. Each of my bridesmaids wore hats and carried a basket of fresh flowers. My youngest cousin was my flower girl and my youngest brother, Knox, was the ring bearer. My sister, Karla, made my wedding gown. The memories that I have from that wedding are from the book of photographs that my mom kept tucked away in one of her closets. I came across these photos while my sister and I were emptying our mom's house to prepare it for sale. Those photos reminded me of that once young girl, who was more focused on the wedding process than she was on the actual marriage that was taking place. I remember being attentive to ensuring that I did everything the way that I thought it was supposed to be done. I registered for our household items at the local department store, I had gathered the necessary items for the ceremony—something old, something new, something borrowed and something blue. Each of these items represented a different aspect of "good luck" for me as the bride. I had no idea how to do marriage, but I wanted to at least appear to others as if I knew what I was doing. When I think back to that time, I can see that I was waiting for someone to rescue me, from myself. Unfortunately, there was no one in my small circle who could rescue me from what I had put into motion, and I did not possess the necessary qualities to help myself. In my "Maggie mind," I thought that if everything was done properly, then the marriage would certainly be a success.

After the wedding ceremony was over, Randy and I walked to the back of the church, as husband and wife. I remember my new father-in-law hugging me and telling me how lucky I was to be a part of their family. He told me I was a "Davis" now and that this was something that I should be proud of! I had a memorable gut reaction when he hugged me and when he said this to me. It was ominous, but I did not understand the reasons why until much later. Awareness of my own gut reactions as intuition was something that I had not yet mastered in my young life.

My new husband had a secret. Randy had grown up in a house ruled by a physically abusive and extremely controlling father. Randy later told me that during his childhood there were many nights when his father would become abusive toward his mother. Randy's reaction was always the same. He would gather his younger brother and sister and put them in the upstairs bedroom, while he sat on the top step of the staircase, waiting for the abuse to end. Hearing this reminded me of how Karla would place all of us in the upstairs closet during my own dad's abusive episodes. Later it would occur to me that children who see violence, often do violence. However, at the time of our wedding, I was unaware of this reality and I was unaware of Randy's secret.

After our wedding celebration, we went to the apartment that we had rented just one street over from my mother's house. Our apartment was located on the first floor. The sequence of events that occurred on that night are a little blurry in my mind, but I had captured most of the highlights in my journal. Randy suddenly became very angry with me. I remember that he had to go to work the next day and he had directed me to pack his lunch. At that time, Randy worked for a construction company and he took his lunch with him every day. He had requested soup for his thermos and so I began to make his lunch. I fixed him a sandwich along with a bag of chips and placed them in his lunch box. I opened a can of condensed soup. I was unaware that milk or water needed to be added to condensed soup in order to thin it out. Believe it or not, I had never fixed a can of condensed soup before that night. Randy saw me trying to pour the thick soup substance into his thermos and he immediately started yelling at me. He called me stupid because I did not know to dilute the soup. He went from a state of anger to rage in a matter of seconds. He became very aggressive towards me and started slapping me around. I was terrified, but I didn't know what to do or who to call. When I was finally able to get to my feet, I quickly ran into our bedroom and locked the door. I knew that Randy could eventually knock down the flimsy bedroom door, so I decided to escape by jumping out the window. I unlocked the bedroom window so that I could leave the apartment. My plan was to run to my mother's house and get my brother, Keith. However, Randy could hear what I was doing inside the bedroom, and he quickly ran out our front door and caught me as I came around the side of our apartment building. He took me back inside our apartment and his fury continued.

Before he came outside to grab me, he had slipped on the steel-toed boots that he wore at his construction job. Eventually his aggression landed me on the floor, huddled in the corner of our hallway. It was at this time that he began to kick me, while I lay in the corner of our hall, crying. After some time had passed, and his fury had spent, he decided to call my girlfriend, Terry. He told her to come and get me, because otherwise he was going to kill me.

Within in thirty minutes, Terry arrived at the doorstop to our apartment. She was crying and clutching her car keys. By that time, the storm that was Randy had calmed. Unfortunately, Terry went home without me. At that time, I did not understand that there would often be a "honeymoon" period after an episode of abuse. The irony was, it actually was our honeymoon, as we had just married a few hours earlier. Randy cried, apologized profusely, and promised that he would never hit me again. Randy lied.

My marriage to Randy lasted only 16 months, but they were 16 of the longest months of my life. I had never worked except for the occasional babysitting in my neighborhood. I went from high school to marriage, from my mother's house to my husband's house. I was expected to be the perfect housewife, but I had no idea how to be one. Eventually, I came to understand that it did not matter how much I cleaned, or how hard I tried to cook, Randy could and would explode at any moment over anything.

We did not live in that apartment for very long. Randy decided that we should save the money that we would otherwise be paying for rent and one day purchase a trailer and perhaps, some land. So, we soon moved into Randy's childhood home, with his parents and younger sister. We did not live with his parents for very long and I have very few memories of the time that we spent living there, with only one exception. As a newly married couple, Randy wanted to have sex almost nightly. There were no locks on our bedroom door and there were many occasions when Randy's dad would burst into the room while we were having sex and then act as if he was unaware that knocking before entering would be preferred. He would linger in our room, making jokes. I was so self-conscious and somewhat scared of Randy's dad. At that time, I still remembered that "weird feeling" that I had experienced when he hugged me in the back of the church after our wedding. His behavior made me very uncomfortable, and I made sure that I was never alone in the house with him. During the time that we lived with Randy's parents, I do not remember Randy having any abusive outbursts towards me. I could tell that he was very uncomfortable around his dad, almost submissive. Eventually I would find out about the abuse that Randy had endured as a child.

Having only gotten married less than two months after graduating high school, I knew little about making a home and even less about making a life. I had never lived on my own. Eventually, Randy's parents helped us purchase a single-wide trailer, which we placed on Randy's uncle's farm, in a rural part of the county. At that time, all of my friends from high school had headed off to college. I felt alone and isolated, living in the country in a trailer, with a boy I hardly knew. It didn't take long for me to realize what a huge mistake marrying Randy really was, but I felt like I had no other options available to me to make a change. I decided that if this was going to be my life, I would make the best of my bad situation. It was unrealistic for me to think that I could somehow make a marriage out of what I had with Randy. Many more life lessons were headed my way before a change would inevitability occur.

I came to cherish my time when Randy was at work. I spent most of my time alone, except for the animals that we had accumulated on our little farm. We had horses, cows, chickens, ducks, and dogs. Shortly before moving to our little farm, my trusted companion, Jeremiah, died. Jeremiah died suspiciously while we were still living at Randy's parents' home and at that time, I had a worrying feeling that his death had not been an accident. However, I had no way to prove anything other than the feelings that I had about the whole event. Randy's father had not been fond of having Jeremiah move into his house with us.

His death occurred while I was not at home with him, and I always suspected that his passing was not accidental, but intentional. After losing Jeremiah, I felt even more alone. I spent a lot of time with my animals because there were very few neighbors who lived around us. We had only one car and Randy drove it to work every day. I'm not sure where my family was at this time, but I had few, if any, visitors. Loneliness became my ever-present companion.

I spent the majority of my time either hiking through the woods on the back part of the property or in the trailer, either cleaning or attempting to fix something for dinner. I did not know much about cooking, as my sister, Karla, had done most of the cooking in our house, and she had not been willing to show me how to cook and I was even less willing to learn. One evening, Randy had been given some deer meat by a friend of his who hunted, and he had told me to fry the meat for dinner. I was not a meat eater, nor was I someone who could cook meat. I really did not know much about cooking at all. I was repulsed to even touch the meat because it was so bloody. That evening, I tried to rinse the meat in the sink, but the sink kept filling up with diluted blood and even then, the meat still looked bloody. I was afraid to not do what Randy had told to me to do, so I eventually put some flour on the meat and placed it in a hot skillet with some oil.

My kitchen sink overlooked our small creek that ran along the side of the property where we lived. I had several ducks that had made a home in my creek, and they were very important to me. As I was washing my bloody hands in the sink, I noticed that all of the ducks were lined up at the edge of the creek, quacking, except for one duck that was thrashing around in the creek. I immediately ran out the door, with absolutely no thought of the deer meat frying on the stove. There was a large snapping turtle in the creek that was trying to pull one of my ducks under the water. I grabbed a shovel from beside the chicken coop and I tried to hit the turtle on the back to make it let go of my duck, but it would not. I then located a stick and stuck it between the turtle's jaws and, finally, the turtle released my duck. This entire rescue mission took approximately 30 minutes. Meanwhile, the deer meat burned on the stove.

Randy came home a short time later and I thought that he would be relieved that I had saved the duck, but he just started yelling at me and then eventually started kicking me around my hips while still wearing his steel-toed work boots. Looking back, he most often kicked or hit me in places that would not usually be visible to others, such as the top of my legs, hips, and arms. He never once hit me on my face.

There are two significant events that stand out during my marriage to Randy and these events serve as a reminder to me of who I was at that time. I once confessed to Randy's mother about his abusive nature towards me because she kept asking me, repeatedly, if he had ever hit me. I eventually told her, yes, he did hit me. I even got really brave and showed her a large bruise on my right hip that covered the entire top part of my leg and hip. She was empathetic because she, too, was an abused wife. I remember that moment, sitting at her kitchen table, when I finally felt some hope that perhaps the nightmare that was my life could end, somehow. I had no idea how it could or would end, but I felt hopeful after telling her my secret. Before I left that day, she gave me an iron skillet that she took off of the top of the stove. She told me to hit Randy with it the next time that he raised a hand to me. After many subsequent talks with Randy's mother, we both began to see an emerging pattern in his abuse towards me. There were times that Randy would stop after work at his parent's home before he came to our house. We both noticed that when he stopped to visit with his parents, he was more likely to come home and take his anger out on me. His mom would call me after he left her house to warn me to protect myself. I never used the skillet for self-defense. It was the same skillet that I had used to burn the deer meat during the duck rescue.

It was on one of these occasions that Randy's mother called to warn me, and I could tell by her voice that this time was different. We were living in the country, and I did not have a car and I did not have time to call anyone. I had never told anyone about Randy's abuse, except for his mother. It was Friday evening and Randy often went to the city on Friday nights to party with his friends who were in a college fraternity. I decided that I would hide out in the woods behind our trailer until Randy got bored with waiting for me. I was hoping that he would eventually leave to go drinking with his friends in Huntington and forget about me. I was scared of the dark but I was even more afraid of Randy's fury. I quickly ran into the woods and hid in an old fox den that I had discovered during one of my many nature hikes on the back of the property where we lived.

Eventually, I heard Randy's loud sports car arrive at our trailer and I held my breath and shut my eyes. I could hear Randy yelling for me, but I didn't answer. There was silence after a while, but I still sat quietly in my hiding place. Then a few moments later I heard Randy's voice again and it was getting closer. Eventually I could hear the heavy breathing of our horse, Sugar. Randy was riding Sugar, bareback, across our pasture while screaming for me to respond. He kept calling my name. He said that I should come out from where ever I was hiding because if I didn't, the bears were going to eat me. Still, I stayed quiet in the fox den. After some time had passed and Randy tired of his search for me, he went back to our trailer. Eventually, I heard him drive away in our car, but still, I stayed for a while longer in the fox den. Randy had left to go drinking with his friends and I eventually returned to our trailer. By then darkness had replaced the light of the day. Randy did not come home that night and by the time he returned the next day, his fury had lessened and he did not mention the events from the previous night.

Towards the end of our marriage, Randy got more and more outrageous with his behavior. He owned a pistol. I was unaware that he had a gun in our home. One day he yelled for me to come to the back door, and I saw him place a bullet in a gun. We were both standing in the narrow hallway of our single-wide trailer, and Randy was holding a gun. I wasn't even shocked that he had a gun. I was so emotionally numb by that time that I had few, if any, emotions about anything. He looked at me and said, "Do you dare me?" I said nothing and I simply stood there. He put the gun to my head and pulled the trigger. I didn't move. The gun did not fire. He then said that he was going to blow my head off, but that he didn't want to make a mess in the trailer, so he opened the back door of our trailer. He pulled the trigger again, but the gun didn't fire, and yet I remained standing there. Getting tired of me, he then pushed me aside and it was over. Randy simply walked away.

Our marriage from that point continued to spiral downhill. Not because I was doing anything different, but because Randy was growing tired of me. He often told me about how many people he had sex with while he was out drinking with his college friends on Friday nights, but still I stayed. I didn't know how to leave. I knew the stigma that my mother endured for being divorced and I was determined to stay in the marriage even if it killed me. I felt that I was totally out of options.

What I didn't know was that God had another plan for my life. One Friday night, Randy came home late and beat me up. I was lying on the couch crying and he was telling me that he didn't love me and that he was going to take me back to my mom's house the following day. I was scared of Randy, but I was also scared to admit to my mom that I had made a huge mistake by marrying him. Randy became more and more aggravated by my crying and started ripping my clothes off. I was screaming, "No, no," but he continued. He raped me that night, while I lay on our couch in our trailer, crying. After he was done with me, he looked right at me and said, "This doesn't change anything. I'm still taking you to your mom's tomorrow." Then he went to our bedroom, closed the door, and went to sleep. I lay there, on the couch, feeling empty and hopeless.

After the rape event, I began to feel an overwhelming calmness inside me that could only have come from God. At that moment, I felt at peace with the ending of my marriage. I was no longer scared to face my mom and for the first time in a long time, I felt hope. I prayed that Randy would still be committed to taking me to my mom's house the following morning.

Randy woke up the next morning and drove me to my girlfriend's house, because I had begged him to not take me to my mom's house. My girlfriend's house was closer, and he stopped the car in the middle of the road in front of my friend's house, leaned across me and threw my small suitcase into the road and told me to get out. That was the end of my marriage to Randy. I spent a few days with my girlfriend before going home to my mom's house.

I lived at my mom's house for a few months. During those few months my eating disorder completely took over. I rapidly lost a lot of weight and eventually weighed a mere 81 pounds. My dad had gotten me a swift divorce with the help of his friend, the "Judge." Because I had only ever had sex with Randy, I believed that he had the right to my body anytime and anywhere he wanted. After a few weeks had passed, Randy began stopping by my mom's house early in the morning on his way home from working the nightshift at the airport. He would have sex with me in the downstairs bathroom of my mother's house. He would then go home, and I would go back to bed. This cycle continued for a few weeks or maybe even months. I do not remember the exact time frame as depression had completely consumed me at that point.

I had never been around any strong women who actually had a voice. It never occurred to me that I could tell him "NO!" During this time, I was shrinking away before my family's eyes, but no one noticed. My mom was busy with her own marriage, my brothers were at that time, all three of them, using alcohol, drugs, and sex to escape their own realities. We were a family in crisis. We were a family of addicts, each acting out in our own way, trying to somehow make our lives bearable.

God had gotten me out of an abusive marriage, but I was not ready to let go of my eating disorder. I had been raised in a house where how a woman looked was important. I remember that my dad would often tell me, after looking at my not too impressive report card, that it was a good thing that I was pretty because I was never going to college. I really believed what he said. I had watched my mom overeat and gain weight since her second marriage and I was determined that would never happen to me. Finally, my eating was something that I could control, or so I thought.

So, my eating disorder became my friend. I never went anywhere without it. There were things that were happening to my body, and I was aware only of the fact that I was losing weight. I had not had a regular menstrual cycle since I had divorced Randy. I was not overly concerned about this fact because I was only focused on losing weight, until I eventually had the thought that I might be pregnant. After four or five months, my periods stopped all together and I became convinced that I was pregnant. By that time, Randy had stopped coming over to my mother's house after he got off work, but we were still having sex, occasionally. One night I went to the airport where Randy worked the nightshift and I told him that I thought that I might be pregnant. We had sex in his office and then I went back home. I don't recall my motive for telling him about my potential pregnancy, but for some reason, I didn't see or hear from him for nearly a year after that night. I suspect that in some way I told Randy so that he could rescue me. At that time in my life, I could not have imagined the person that I would eventually learn to become. Eventually, I would learn to rescue myself.

There were only two people who knew about my pregnancy suspicion. Pam, a friend from the department store where I worked, in whom I had confided, and Terry, my best friend whom Randy had called on the night of our honeymoon. It was 1976, and abortion was illegal in West Virginia. I believed that there was a stigma that went along with having an abortion. Abortion was considered the greatest sin, according to my church. I knew that Randy was gone forever, and I had no means with which to provide for a baby. I was terrified.

At that time, I made the only decision that I could make. I made the decision to have an abortion. Terry took me to an abortion clinic in Cincinnati, Ohio. My friend, Pam, covered for me at work with my employer. I was waiting at the clinic with Terry when, finally, my name was called. After being taken back to a small examination room, the counselor told me that my pregnancy test, done that day, was inconclusive and that they could not perform an abortion on me as previously planned. It was a Wednesday. I was sent home with five pills that I was told to take on Saturday. I was told to come back to the clinic the following week if my period had not started. I waited until Saturday and I took the pills, as instructed, around noon. I did not know what kind of pills they were and I did not really care; I just wanted the whole pregnancy nightmare to end.

About five hours after I had taken the pills, I became violently ill. Two of my brothers were home with me at my mom's house and all three of us became very concerned for my welfare. Eventually they had to rush me to the hospital. I didn't tell my brothers about the pills that I had taken earlier that day. At the hospital I was triaged to a room immediately, because of the severity of my condition. After the nurse was done with her initial assessment, I was left alone in the room for what seemed like a long time. I was having severe abdominal cramping and I was vomiting continuously. Finally, a young man came in wearing a white jacket, and he sat down on the edge of my bed. I had a strange feeling when he did not introduce himself to me, but I assumed that he was a doctor. He asked me what was wrong, and I began to tell him the whole story. He said, "So, you think you're pregnant?" I timidly said, "Yes." He slipped off my gown and I assumed that he was going to examine me. Instead, he leaned forward and with both his hands he began squeezing and fondling my breasts. I stayed very still as fear and nausea took over my body. Nausea won, as I quickly leaned forward and vomited on one of his shoes. I apologized as he angrily stood up and left the room. I never saw him again. Later a female doctor came in and told me that the pills that I had taken were birth control pills, meant to start my period. She sent me home and told me that if I did not start my period in the next forty-eight hours that I should assume that I was pregnant. I went home and I didn't tell anyone what happened in the hospital, not even my brothers.

My period never came and the following Friday, Terry, and I, again, made the trip from West Virginia to Cincinnati, Ohio to the abortion clinic. This time they were prepared to perform the procedure. I paid them my three hundred and twenty-five dollars and waited for my name to be called. When it was my turn, I stood up like a robot and walked through the doors. I took off all my clothes and I put on a gown. I was lying on a hard table in a small room while someone was putting an intravenous line into my arm. I kept my eyes focused on the ceiling. I had to concentrate on something because if I thought for one minute about my baby, I knew that I would run away as fast as I could. My nurse came in and she introduced herself but, still, I kept my eyes on the ceiling. Everything went quickly from that point. I began to feel drowsy and I could feel my legs being placed in the stirrups as the nurse was telling the doctor that we were ready. She stood beside me, gently squeezing my hand. The last thing that I remembered before I drifted off to sleep was that I glanced over at the nurse who had so tenderly taken my hand, and I saw her full round belly, pregnant with her own baby. She was smiling down at me. With tears welling up in my eyes as I looked at her belly, I felt my own legs in the stirrups, and I went to sleep.

When I woke up, I was in a room filled with small cots and rows of other women who had just experienced what I had. The nurse came over to me and explained to me what had happened. She told me that I had indeed been pregnant, probably about five or six months, but that the baby had died a long time ago. She said that ordinarily my body would have expelled the contents of my uterus but for some reason this had not happened. She then explained that this was why my previous pregnancy test came back as inconclusive. She described this as a "missed abortion." The whole time she was talking, all I could think about was that I had to get out of there. I was beginning to panic! Before they would let me leave the clinic, they had to have a discussion with me about birth control which I declined to take. I had to sign a document stating that birth control was explained to me in detail and that I had declined to accept. In my "Maggie mind" I was never going to have sex again.

The idea of having sex with more than one person, on top of being divorced and having had an abortion, was unfathomable to me. It made me sound like the kind of person that I pretended not to be, not to mention the fact that I knew that several of these attributes were in the "sin book" of my childhood Baptist Church. I could not imagine a lower point in my life.

Terry took me home and we never spoke of the baby again. I ached for my baby. I ached for the person that I wanted to be. I had terminated my relationship with Randy at the same time that I terminated my baby. All I had left was an eating disorder to distract me from all the intense feelings that I was having. For a while, it was enough. Eventually, not even my eating disorder could contain the agony that I felt inside me. The multitude of feelings that I began to feel were often too much for me to even process. I had absolutely no idea how I was ever going to move forward with my life. Prior to the abortion, I had confessed to my mom that I was pregnant with Randy's baby. She never made eye contact with me as she said, "You've made your bed, now you can lie in it." We never spoke of it again. I often pretended with my "Maggie mind" that it wasn't even real, but the reality of what had happened would always seep back in and I would again be reminded of my baby over and over again. The abortion was the impetus for moving from my mother's house into my own apartment with my girlfriend. My eating disorder buffered the pain from my abortion, but I had a long road ahead of me and it would be many years before I forgave myself for the abortion and for marrying Randy in the first place. Healing the wounds that were left inside of me were still a long way away. And while I was learning to notice the "weird feeling" I would get around certain people and situations; I would have to experience many more lessons before I would learn to trust myself, enough, to act on it. Looking back, there were so many warning signs, and I see now how much pain I could have avoided if only I had trusted myself and those gut feelings. It would be my life's journey to learn to trust my deep, inner knowing, to have more respect and love for myself and to create boundaries with others. To honor myself in body, mind, and spirit.

LESSON FOUR

Often, lessons learned in childhood must be unlearned in adulthood

What is it about childhood that causes everything to cling to us like Velcro? Every challenge I've faced in therapy can be directly linked to an experience from my early years. I am afraid of the dark. Even now as I write this, I can understand how absurd it is for a grown woman with grown children to be afraid of the dark. My earliest memory of darkness was when I was a small child around three years of age.

My sister and I were sitting in the back seat of our dad's big Buick convertible, with the top down, and our dad had parked us beside a large tree. He left us there and told us to stay in the car, which we did. I can't remember if he ran out of gas or if we were parked close to a bar, but if I had to pick one, I would say he found a bar. Darkness eventually swallowed up the day as my sister and I sat on the floor of the backseat just wishing for the sunlight to appear.

Wishing for light became a theme for my life. Moving towards the light, holding the light, seeing the light – light was all I wanted in my life. I have never lived alone and even the thought of living alone would always make me feel afraid, which, again would reminded me of darkness. This was the cycle that turned over and over in my head. I moved from my mother's house at 18 years of age to an abusive marriage, from darkness to darkness.

My father was a sex addict, and my mother had an eating disorder. I learned as a young child that people were judged by their appearance. My father frequently commented to me that all I would be good for was to get married and have babies. In other words, what I learned from my father was that my worth as a woman, was directly connected to my uterus and my ability to have children. This lesson would consume 18 years of my marriage to my second husband, Jay.

In 1994, I was in my second year of my PhD program, when I had a surprise pregnancy confirmed at approximately 15 weeks' gestation. I went for my initial obstetric appointment and after my examination, I was sent to the appointment secretary's desk so that all the appropriate tests could be scheduled. I was thirty-eight years old, and Jay and I had been married for 16 years. The secretary looked at my chart and noticed that the number "10" was written in the space meant for the number of pregnancies, inclusive of the current pregnancy. She asked me to correct the number "10," located in the upper right-hand corner of the form. I looked at her and said, "The number is correct, this is my 10th pregnancy." She looked at me with total disbelief.

Ten pregnancies are a lot for one body, and in 1994 I was pregnant for the tenth time. There were times that even I was amazed by the number 10. I had spent my entire adulthood playing out a painful lesson that I learned as a child. My worth was linked to my body, specifically to my uterus. When I married Jay, the same feelings of unworthiness would creep back into my mind, and I would again start to question myself: Am I worthy enough to be married to Jay? Am I worthy enough to be accepted by my mother in-law? Am I worthy?

I had experienced a lot of guilty feelings about the abortion that I had after I divorced my first husband, Randy. Even though that baby had already died several weeks before the abortion was completed, I still carried a lot of shame about the fact that I had made the decision to have an abortion. When I married Jay in 1978, I wanted to get pregnant as soon as possible. We never used birth control, but it still took us almost three years to get pregnant with our first child. We were actually in the process of being evaluated for infertility when Karter was finally conceived. It was 1981, I had only recently started college at the age of 25 and Jay was, at that time, enrolled in medical school. We were living in a small town in southern West Virginia while we were both attending college in Huntington at Marshall University.

Both of our families were thrilled about our upcoming pregnancy! Secretly, I was relieved that God was not going to punish me for having had an abortion several years prior. At that time in my life, I still believed in my childhood Baptist doctrine that I had been taught throughout my life. Abortion was a sin and God punished sinners. These were the teachings of my church.

My pregnancy with Karter was difficult and there were times that I was convinced that I was being punished for what I had done to my first baby. I experienced bleeding several times throughout the pregnancy. Every time I used the bathroom and saw blood on the tissue, I became consumed with terror. I was in a constant state of fear at the thought of losing my pregnancy. I was frequently placed on bed rest restrictions by my obstetrician, but to our surprise, the pregnancy continued. When I was in my fifth month of pregnancy (around 20 weeks' gestation), I was hospitalized due to some preterm labor symptoms that began causing cervical changes. My obstetrician worried that these symptoms might trigger a preterm delivery. It was 1981, and at that time preterm infants had a very low survival rate. Ritodrine was the only drug that was approved by the Food and Drug Administration (FDA) for suppression of premature labor, and it was not available in the state of West Virginia and had never been used anywhere in the state. My obstetrician knew about the drug and contacted a colleague at a hospital in Virginia to request access to the drug. He was finally able to order the drug from the hospital at the University of Virginia. All we had to do was wait for this new miracle drug to arrive.

We knew that our baby had little to no chance of survival if I delivered at a gestation of only twenty weeks. Knowing that there was a new treatment that might help me carry my baby to term was all that we could think about. At the time of this hospitalization, we knew that we were having a boy. Initially, I did not think about the fact that the staff at our hospital might be inexperienced with the administration of this new drug. I was just focused on saving our baby. When the drug finally arrived at the hospital, the nurse manager came in my room to tell us that the pharmacy had just received the drug and that they were in the process of preparing the drug for my administration. Jay and I were both elated. We were so connected to this little baby.

Jay was in the room with me when the doctor and two nurses came in to start the drug administration. Jay was standing at the end of my bed when the nurse started the infusion of the drug through my intravenous line, which had been in place since I was initially admitted to the hospital. I immediately began to feel tingly all over. I had an electronic blood pressure cuff on my right arm, which gave my blood pressure readings every two minutes. Everything that happened next, happened without my having any concept of the passage of time because within two minutes of the beginning of the infusion, I slipped into unconsciousness. The last words I remember hearing were, "Her pressure is dropping. It's at 40!" The tingling sensation remained in my body as I began to slowly drift away.

The following events occurred during an out of body experience that I had after I drifted off into unconsciousness. Suddenly, my body was hovering near the ceiling, and I could see myself lying in the bed below. I could not hear any sounds, but I could see everything that was happening in the room. There were about 20 people frantically running in and out of my room. Clearly, the code blue emergency alert had been activated, as the crash cart (a wheeled container carrying medicine and equipment for emergency resuscitations) was brought into my room. Jay was standing against the wall at the foot of my bed. He looked frozen in terror. I am not sure why they did not ask him to leave the room, which would have been standard procedure in such an event. But whether it was the chaos that quickly engulfed the room or the fact that Jay was by then in medical school, he saw everything that happened. I too, watched as everyone tried to revive me. They immediately stopped the infusion of the medication, but my blood pressure was not responding. I was not feeling any pain, and I could not hear any sound. I remember feeling an urgency within myself as I looked again at the person who was lying on the bed below me. I saw the little belly bump under the white sheet and I thought about my unborn son, Karter. I felt like at that point I had a choice to make about whether or not to return to my body. It was an easy choice: I chose Karter. During this experience, I had no concept of time. I suddenly opened my eyes to find myself looking up at the frantic face of my nurse who was visibly relieved to see me open my eyes.

My "out of body" experience terrified me. I did not tell anyone about it for several years, not even Jay. When I finally recounted the sequence of events that I had witnessed during my unconscious state, Jay was speechless. They were the same events that he had witnessed while standing in the room when they had occurred.

After this incident, my doctor decided to give me the Ritodrine medication orally. I stayed in the hospital for another two weeks, so that I could be closely monitored while taking the drug by mouth. After being discharged from the hospital, I was put on complete bedrest until the end of the pregnancy. At that time, Jay and I lived in a second-story apartment. Because of my bedrest restrictions, we made the decision to move in with his parents. I was allowed to get out of bed to use the bathroom and to go to my weekly doctor appointments. Otherwise, I was totally confined to the bed. At times, the restrictions were hard to maintain, but I was determined to deliver my son safely and I did exactly as I was instructed. Jay and I stayed with his parents until I was in my 38th week of pregnancy, before moving back to our apartment. The week that we moved back to our apartment was when Karter decided to come into this world. It was June 24, 1981. The labor was long, but the results were worth every minute. I finally had the baby that I had yearned for all my life and I had proven my worth to everyone – at least that's what I had initially thought.

Somehow the local news station was informed about the use of the new drug, Ritodrine, in a Huntington hospital that successfully delayed a potential preterm delivery and produced a healthy term infant. Before we left the hospital, the television crew came to the hospital and did a brief interview with Jay and I, with Karter being featured on the local 6 p.m. news. Our families were thrilled!

Ritodrine was eventually taken off the market by United States Food and Drug Administration (FDA) in 1998 for the prevention of preterm delivery. Reasons cited for removal of the drug were due to severe maternal side effects such as cardiovascular complications and death. However, before the drug was removed from the market, I would have one more experience with taking this drug for yet a subsequent pregnancy.

In 1982, we learned that I was pregnant again. Jay and I had decided to wait to tell our families about the pregnancy. Jay was busy with interviews for his residency, as he was about to finish medical school. I didn't mind not telling anyone because it felt sacred that only Jay and I knew about our new baby. While Jay was out of town wrapping up his residency interviews, I began to bleed. Throughout the evening, the bleeding increased, and I began to experience severe abdominal pains. I was home alone with my young son, Karter. At some point during the night, while I was in the bathroom doubled over in pain, I expelled a large mass of blood and tissue into the toilet. In that moment, I realized that my baby had died. I was home alone. I flushed the toilet and spent most of that night crying for the loss of my baby. Karter was in his crib sleeping. After it was all over, I went over to stare at him lying in his bed, sleeping. At that time, I was still in nursing school, and I was scheduled to be in the operating room (OR) that morning at 7:30 a.m. It was well past 3 a.m. before I went to bed. I tucked my feelings deep inside me so that I could get on with the day ahead of me.

Morning came very quickly. I rushed to get Karter ready to take him to my mother's house, so that she could watch him while I was in school all day. The events of the previous night were still heavy on my mind and on my physical body. The physical impact of experiencing a miscarriage was as difficult as the psychological burden of losing our baby. Because we had made the decision to not tell our families about the new baby, I had also not told the leadership in my nursing program. I just thought that I could power my way forward through the day. I arrived at the hospital on time and was immediately instructed on how to gown and scrub to prepare for my day in the surgery suite. There were three students, including myself, in the surgical suite that day. I was standing in the middle, between my other two classmates, after we had all properly scrubbed in. The lead OR nurse had placed us on a small platform so that we could view the abdominal surgery that was scheduled to occur first. The surgeon came in and the OR team prepared to start the surgery. The patient was draped, and the surgeon prepared to make the initial incision into the abdomen. As the scalpel moved down the abdomen toward the naval and the skin began to peel apart, I fainted.

I have no memory of anything that was said or even how I was removed from the surgical suite. I was later scolded by my professor for my inappropriate behavior in the OR. I never told anyone about my miscarriage the night before.

In 1983, I became pregnant again and we were tentatively thrilled. Jay was graduating from medical school, and I was graduating from nursing school in May of that year. In February, I began to spot, and my doctor put me on complete bedrest. The bleeding continued until Jay eventually had to take me to the hospital. When we arrived at the hospital, I had a sonogram that confirmed the death of our baby. I had surgery to remove the contents of my pregnant uterus. This was what my doctor called it, but to me, it was surgery to remove my dead baby. I was devastated. Feelings of worthlessness consumed me, and I was convinced that Karter would be our only child.

In 1984, I became pregnant again. Jay and I had relocated after college to north-central Kentucky. Jay was completing his residency program in pediatrics, and I was working in a private pediatric practice as a registered nurse. Moving away from West Virginia was very difficult for me. I had never considered that moving would be an option for me, but my marriage to Jay opened many possibilities for me that I had initially resisted. Jay loved to travel, and I did not. I had not been brought up to see my potential beyond the small town where I was raised. Our move to Kentucky turned out to be a very positive move for us as a family. This was where we would purchase our first home and where we immediately immersed ourselves in our new community. Jay's residency kept him very busy, but we were so excited to have another baby on the way. The pregnancy with Karson proceeded without any complications. I worked up until I went to labor at thirty-eight weeks and I even gained 70 pounds! My sister, Karla, had come to visit us for the weekend when I suddenly went into labor on Sunday morning August 12, 1984, the same day she had planned on returning home. However, in perfect "Karla fashion," she extended her stay with us so that she could take care of Karter when we went to the hospital. I was so proud to have successfully done pregnancy the right way and I was anticipating being rewarded with another beautiful son. The mindset of the Baptist Church rhetoric of reward and punishment was still prevalent in my mind.

My mother-in-law had let me know early in our marriage how much she wanted me to have a little girl with dark hair. We knew early in the pregnancy that Karson was a boy, but we had decided to not tell our families because we wanted them to be surprised. When I went into labor, Jay's parents made the drive from West Virginia to Kentucky, while I was laboring at the hospital. By the time they arrived, Karson had already been born. I could hear Jay's parents in the hall asking for my room number. I could hear the nurse leading them down the hall to my room and I heard Jay's mom ask the nurse if I had had a girl or a boy. The nurse said, "She can tell you." All my mother-in-law heard was the word "she" and she excitedly said, "Oh, she had a girl!" As they entered my room, I looked at my mother-in-law and immediately said, "Mom, it's a boy." My mother-in-law patted my leg as she entered and said, "That's okay, you'll do better next time." I know that she meant for those words to comfort me, however, I felt those old feelings of worthlessness fill my body, once again.

Right after Karson was born and before anyone from either of our families had arrived, Jay and I had a precious moment of time together, just the three of us. I was lying in my bed with Karson lying on my chest, swaddled in my arms and Jay was hovering over our bed as we both marveled at the huge blessing that we had received with his birth. That was such a precious time for me. When I think back and remember times in my life where love consumed me, I remember this moment.

I went back to school in 1986 to get my baccalaureate degree in nursing. It was a very stressful time. I was working full time, going to school full time and breastfeeding Karson. I discovered that I was pregnant in April of 1986. I was convinced that I had been cured of any possibility of a miscarriage since my pregnancy with Karson had gone so smoothly. When I started spotting, I became terrified. However, the sonogram showed a healthy baby, and I was, again, relieved. Then just one week later the second sonogram showed something was wrong. I could see the look on the technician's face as she scanned my belly. I asked if everything was all right and she just patted my hand, but she didn't say anything else to me. She quickly left the room and a few minutes later, a doctor appeared with her that I had never seen before. He leaned over to view the image on the monitor and then he patted my hand and said, "Your baby has no heartbeat," and then he left. Again, I had surgery to remove the contents of my pregnant uterus. There was no surgery available to remove the contents of my broken heart.

I got pregnant again just six months after my fourth baby had died. This pregnancy followed the same path as the previous one and just five weeks before Christmas, I had surgery to remove the contents of my pregnant uterus. As I was lying on the table, being prepped for surgery, the nurse carefully placed my legs in the stirrups as I was staring up at the ceiling. I had been in this place before. I had walked into the hospital pregnant and within three hours I would walk out not pregnant. As I was drifting off to sleep, the nurse commented that this time they were going to find out why my body was having so much difficulty carrying my pregnancies to term.

At that time, it was recommended that after a woman experienced a total of 3 miscarriages, she needed to be worked up medically to try and decipher the underlying cause or causes for the miscarriages. After my most recent loss, my physician did a workup on me and the only thing that resulted was that perhaps I needed to take supplemental progesterone during my pregnancies to keep the uterus from expelling the fetus. Progesterone supplementation is not routinely recommended for recurrent pregnancy loss but some studies in the research literature suggest a potential benefit in reducing the miscarriage risk, while other studies have been inconclusive about the efficacy of its use. For me, I felt that it was worth a try and the decision was made that with each subsequent pregnancy I would use the progesterone supplementation until I had completed 16 full weeks of pregnancy. I was elated to be given even a glimmer of hope that Jay and I would be able to have another successful pregnancy after experiencing so many losses.

Miscarriage is one of those medical mysteries that physicians like to discount as God's way of destroying an unhealthy baby. The truth is that women who have experienced miscarriages see them very differently. The grief of miscarriage is often complicated by many factors. For me, the lack of acknowledgement that my babies were real and the absence of any memories, such as a lock of hair, movement, or even knowing the gender of my babies, complicated my own passage through grief. In my mind, the greatest grief was that my body had deceived me over and over again and was not functioning like all the other women in the world. I know that this seems like an unrealistic perception, but at that time my reality was distorted. The feelings of unworthiness that I carried throughout my childhood into adulthood skewed my perception of my pregnancies.

The grief of miscarriage consumed a lot of my life and even directed both my master's thesis and my doctorate dissertation many years later. While completing the work for my dissertation, I started a support group for parents who had experienced miscarriage. I ran this support group for several years, and the lessons I learned from the couples involved in the support group helped me narrow the focus for my doctorate dissertation exclusively on the father's experience of miscarriage. The fathers in my groups talked about how their initial focus after a miscarriage was to always concentrate, exclusively, on relieving the suffering of their spouse. They expressed that their own grief seemed to lag behind that of their spouse's grief. Delayed grieving for fathers has been documented in the research literature and is cited as one of the main reasons that the divorce rate is higher for couples after a loss.

On several occasions I had tried to talk with Jay about our many miscarriages, but he was never able to articulate any feelings, thoughts or emotions related to how he felt about our losses. I wanted so desperately to understand Jay's experience with our miscarriages. The fathers who participated in my doctoral research were very open with me about their miscarriage experiences. These fathers' experiences provided me with a glimpse into the paternal response after miscarriage. By the time I had completed my research for my doctoral dissertation and published my findings, Jay and I had divorced. To this day, he and I have never talked about his experiences with any of our many miscarriages.

In 1988, Jay had finished his residency and his fellowship, I had completed my bachelor's degree in nursing, and we prepared our family for our upcoming move to northeast Mississippi. Jay was convinced that he had found his perfect place to practice. The move to Mississippi was not what I wanted, but I said nothing. Initially, the two places that Jay had given me as possibilities for our next move included a small town in Mississippi or Minot, North Dakota. We actually took a trip to Minot to check out the area but we both decided, almost immediately, that moving to such a cold climate would be our last choice. Therefore, the decision was made for us – Mississippi it was! Just a few weeks before we were scheduled to move, I found out that I was pregnant. I was so excited. I was convinced that God was going to give me a baby as a gift, because I had to move to Mississippi. I was sure that I would carry this new baby to term, especially now that I was taking the progesterone supplements. But I was mistaken.

Soon after we moved to Mississippi, Jay found me an obstetrician named John. After my initial visit, John sent me for an ultrasound. The technician did a vaginal sonogram to help get a better view of the baby, but she was unable to find anything on the scan. She comforted me and told me not to worry because I was only a few weeks pregnant. She suggested that perhaps the baby had not yet implanted into the uterus. After that ultrasound, I went back into the dressing room. I remember starring at my naked reflection in the mirror, focusing directly on the place where my baby should have been growing. I started to cry. Over the next week I had two or three additional ultrasounds but still Nina, the technician, could not find any evidence of a fetus with a heartbeat.

Eleven days after we moved to Mississippi, I began to have severe pain on my left side. It was the worst pain that I had ever experienced. I knew in an instant that something was seriously wrong. Jay took me immediately to his hospital. I was utterly mortified to meet, for the first time, all of his colleagues while I lay on the stretcher, screaming. It felt like my body was exploding from the inside. John, my obstetrician, ordered another sonogram, but it was difficult for the technician to visualize anything. Then I heard John exclaim, "There's the fetus, it's extrauterine!" I knew that "extrauterine" meant that my baby was not growing in the uterus. I stated screaming, "No, no!" I wasn't screaming because I overheard them mention that I required immediate surgery because my left fallopian tube, where my baby was currently located, was on the verge of rupturing. I was crying because I knew that another one of my babies was going to die. At that point, I wanted to die.

After my sixth baby died, I became obsessed with pregnancy. I was determined to have another baby even if it killed me. I convinced my husband, Jay, to write me a prescription for the fertility pill, Clomid. Clomid creates an artificial low-estrogen environment in the brain, thereby prompting the body to produce more of the hormones needed to stimulate the ovaries and trigger ovulation. In other words, it causes the body to produce more than one egg per cycle, thereby increasing a woman's chances of becoming pregnant and becoming pregnant with multiples. After my surgery from the ectopic pregnancy, I started taking Clomid before I even had a normal menstrual cycle. It is usually recommended that a woman wait three to six months after a miscarriage before trying again to become pregnant. I had not grieved the loss of my sixth baby. I tucked it away deep inside me so that I could concentrate on having another baby. Seven weeks after I got out of the hospital with my most recent pregnancy loss, I was pregnant again. It was October 11, 1988.

Due to my complicated prenatal history, my obstetrician sent me to a perinatal specialist in Memphis because he felt unqualified to follow me through another potentially difficult pregnancy. The perinatal specialist was Dr. Carson. She was experienced with pregnancy histories such as mine and she immediately put me at ease. She talked so matter of fact about everything that I began to believe that I was actually going to carry this new baby.

The first thing that Dr. Carson wanted to do was to draw blood to test my progesterone level. Progesterone is the hormone that inhibits the uterine wall from sloughing off so that the pregnancy can be maintained. Dr. Carson had already explained to me that a level below 6.5 would indicate that I would most likely be unable to carry the baby. She reiterated that a level above 6.5 would indicate the best chance of carrying this new baby to term. After arriving back home from my visit, the hospital called me with my results, my level was 6.5, not 6.4 or 6.6, but 6.5. Dr. Carson had explained the probable outcome if my level was below 6.5 or above 6.5, but not for 6.5! It was a Friday, and I cried all weekend, just waiting for the blood to appear on the tissue, indicating another miscarriage, but it never happened. I was scheduled to see Dr Carson every week, and the following week I made the 85-mile trip to Memphis for my weekly sonogram. I had convinced myself that I was carrying yet another dead baby, but surprisingly, there was a heartbeat! I couldn't understand how this baby was still alive since my progesterone level was only 6.5. Dr. Carson came in to examine me and I asked her how long it would be before the baby would die, given that my progesterone level was so low. She acted as if she didn't know what I was talking about and when I told her that someone from her office had called me the previous week and told me that my progesterone level was 6.5, she immediately began searching through my chart for the lab results. Obviously, she knew nothing about the lab results and as I was preparing myself for the bad news, she said "Kim, your level wasn't 6.5, it was 65. They must have put the decimal point in the wrong place. Your pregnancy is progressing fine!" Decimal point in the wrong place! That seemed like a logical enough explanation, but

I was devastated. I had already come to terms with the fact that I was going to lose yet another baby and now I wasn't. I was afraid to be happy. I was trying to prepare myself for the inevitable death of yet another baby.

Three weeks passed without incidence. I was having two sonograms per week: one in Mississippi and one in Memphis. The baby was growing, and everything looked normal. Then I woke up on a Sunday morning and I was bleeding– not spotting, but bleeding. I assumed that this would be the end of my pregnancy. I called Dr Carson and told her that my pregnancy was ending. She didn't believe that the pregnancy was ending, as she had just seen me two days prior, but deep down I felt certain I was losing the baby. Dr. Carson wanted me to come to her office the following morning so that she could do another sonogram and take a biopsy of the fetus to check, if, indeed, I was in the process of aborting the baby. My grief was so intense, it completely engulfed my body. I was almost inconsolable. Jay was always uncomfortable with my emotional state and this time he convinced me to take a valium tablet to help calm me down. The reality is that Jay felt uneasy about me experiencing any emotions, particularly the sad ones. The next morning Jay went with me to Memphis. On the way, an overwhelming calmness came over me (maybe it was the Valium) and I told Jay that I felt that the baby had not died after all. Jay snapped back with, "You know the baby is dead!" We had been through so much loss in our marriage that we were both afraid to have hope. I did not say anything else, but I felt God telling me that our baby was going to be okay.

We went straight to the ultrasound room and the technician inserted the probe into my vagina and slowly we saw our baby come into focus. His heart was beating! I cried with joy as I watched my son sleeping safely inside me. Jay and I were both stunned, but ecstatic.

Two weeks later, the ultrasound technician discovered a large blood clot that had formed inside my uterus. Dr Carson told us that if my body did not absorb the clot, that it was large enough to cause me to lose the pregnancy. I went home and I sat up for three days and two nights. I was afraid that if I laid down, the clot might move and cause my baby to die. The week before Thanksgiving, the clot finally began to shrink. We were filled, once more, with hope. The following week I would be 12 weeks pregnant. This would be the last time I would see Dr Carson as she felt that I could then be safely followed by my regular obstetrician, John, in Mississippi. Jay and I were excited to be over the crisis part of the pregnancy. We decided to take our other two sons with us for our last appointment in Memphis, so that they could see their new brother, Kaiden, on the sonogram screen.

During the ultrasound, the technician did very little talking, but we barely noticed as we were busy chatting with our boys, trying to point out their new brother growing inside of me. Suddenly, Dr. Carson entered the room. She had been reviewing the ultrasound remotely from another room. She explained that our baby was currently in heart failure. His ventricles were beating over three hundred beats per minute, and the atrial response was around forty. We were told that our baby would be dead within forty-eight hours if they did not intervene immediately. I was rushed to the hospital. Meanwhile, Jay left so that he could take our boys back to Mississippi and try to find someone to cover his practice before returning to Memphis to be with me and our baby. I was admitted to the labor and delivery wing of the University Hospital in Memphis, and I shared a bathroom with a woman who quickly gave birth, as I listened from my room. Jay was unable to come back to the hospital that day, so I was alone in my hospital room in Memphis. I had several specialists come in to talk with me to give me their opinions about Kaiden's condition, along with his chances of survival. The chances of my carrying our baby to term ranged from 20 to 40 percent. The truth was that there had never been a successful cardio-conversion of a baby's heartbeat at only 12 gestational weeks. At that time the earliest known cardio-conversion documented in the research literature was at 18 weeks' gestation. However, everyone concurred that without a cardio-conversion, the pregnancy would be lost.

It was Friday. They loaded me with the medicine, Digoxin, which was meant to slow our baby's heartbeat to a normal rate. The side effect of the medicine was that it slowed my heartbeat as well. On Sunday morning, they did an ultrasound to check Kaiden's progress. Another miracle had touched our son – his heart was beating normally. On Monday morning another ultrasound was done, and his heart was still beating normally. It was then that the doctors told me that a sack of fluid had formed around the back of his head called a "hygroma" and that I should be prepared for the fact that our baby could be born with a genetic defect. A hygroma in utero (during pregnancy) means that the lymphatic system (a network of vessels that collect fluid from the body and return it to the blood stream, helping to maintain fluid balance) is not developing correctly, leading to the presence of fluid-filled sacs. These sacs are typically benign but can be associated with genetic abnormalities.

I was only 12 weeks pregnant, and the pain in my heart for my baby filled every cell in my body. On Tuesday, December 16th, I was scheduled for an amniocentesis. The fluid around the back of Kaiden's head had remained evident since my discharge from the Memphis hospital several weeks prior, but on that day, as the doctor was preparing to do the procedure, he was unable to locate any fluid. We found out on the Friday before Christmas that the genetic testing showed that Kaiden was a normal healthy boy. Nothing was going to touch our son now. I was determined to take this baby to term. I had to stay on the medicine to keep his heart beating normally. We purchased an ultrasound stethoscope so that I could monitor his heartbeat daily. We had become so attached to this baby. It felt as though we had fought a war, but it had been worth all the pain to have our son safe inside of me.

I went into premature labor on February 27th, but I was successfully given medication to stop the labor. I was given Ritodrine, the same medication that I had used during my pregnancy with my first son, Karter. It was 1989, nine years before the drug would be taken off the market by the FDA. Due to my previous experience with the drug in 1981, it was decided to only use the oral dose instead of starting with the intravenous dose. Each time they tried to decrease the dosage or change the timing of the dose, I would immediately start having contractions again. After a two-week stay in the hospital, the decision was made to take the medicine every two hours around the clock to keep from going into labor. I was already taking Digoxin to keep Kaiden from going into heart failure, along with the Ritodrine every two hours to decrease the chances of delivering prematurely. The combination of these two drugs left me feeling very ill for the remaining months of the pregnancy. I weighed only 116 pounds on the day that I finally went into labor at 39 weeks' gestation.

Kaiden's original due date was my husband's birthday, June 9th. I finally made it to June. I was induced on June 6, 1989. Initially, my labor progressed well. Then I started having a feeling that the baby was not tolerating the labor. I told my husband on several occasions that something was wrong, but Jay kept reassuring me that everything was fine. But then it wasn't.

Kaiden's heart rate dropped, without warning. At that point, I had been trying to have a natural childbirth and I did not have an intravenous line in place. My obstetrician, John, was at my bedside, constantly. I knew that something was terribly wrong because he had not left my bedside. They had turned off the volume for the fetal monitor so that I could not hear that my baby's heart was not recovering after each contraction. Suddenly, my room was filled with people and chaos took over the room. I was asking someone, anyone, to tell me what was happening. Suddenly, my abdomen was being prepped for surgery. Someone was trying to get an access line placed in my arm while they were wheeling me quickly to the operating room. As soon as I got to the operating room, I saw Dr. Jones. He had been the anesthesiologist when I had the ruptured fallopian tube surgery just a few months prior. I was crying and begging someone to save my baby. Dr. Jones touched my shoulder and said, "This time we are going to get you a baby!"

I was not numb. I could feel everything that everyone was doing to my body. I told John, my obstetrician, that I could still feel everything. He was scrubbed and I saw that he was holding the scalpel over my abdomen. I was so afraid that he was going to cut me before I went to sleep. That was my last memory......

I had to have an emergency cesarean section. Kaiden had struggled to enter this world, but no baby was ever so wanted or so loved as this one. When I started to wake up after the surgery, I had this fear that my husband, Jay, was trying to kill me. I was feeling very paranoid and as I started to arouse, I could hear myself making noises and then I could hear Jay telling the nurse that I was in pain, and he would then instruct her to give me more sedation. I remember feeling terrified and I even devised a plan in my mind where I would slowly awaken without making a sound or a movement until I was fully awake so that I could stop Jay from sedating me. The reality of that situation was that the medicine that I was taking was causing extreme paranoia and Jay was just trying to keep me comfortable after an extremely traumatic delivery.

Kaiden was almost two years old before I asked Jay to tell me about his delivery. I told Jay that I had almost no memory of anything after seeing the scalpel in John's hand, as he was standing over my abdomen, and I also knew that it had taken me two days to awaken after the surgery, which was way outside of the normal range. Jay responded, "I have been waiting for you to ask me, so that I could tell you what happened."

Jay began to share. He told me that because I did not already have an intravenous line in place, it took the team some time before they could get access and give me the sedation needed for the surgery. John, the obstetrician, made the decision that he could no longer wait for me to be sedated because Kaiden was in heart failure and had to be delivered immediately in order to save his life. They had several people in the OR (operating room) lay on top of me to hold me down while John started my surgery without my being fully sedated. Jay told me that I was screaming and fighting against the weight that was holding me in place. The surgery continued. He said that after what seemed like forever, my screaming stopped as the sedation was slowly taking over my body. Kaiden was delivered and rushed immediately to the Neonatal Intensive Care Unit (NICU), and Jay had gone to the NICU with him. Jay told me that the anesthesiologist, Dr. Jones, and my OBGYN, John, decided together to give me some medication that would induce mild amnesia so that the memories of what had happened in the OR would not be part of Kaiden's birth story.

I did not even think about having another baby for years and even then, the thought would enter my mind and then quickly, I would dismiss it. I was terrified to ever get pregnant again. I had started to work on my doctorate degree in 1993. In the spring of 1994, I had the same dream three times, while I was away at school in Charlottesville. In the dream I was on the stage receiving my doctorate degree and as I looked out in the audience, I saw my children standing so proudly as my name was called. Karter, my oldest son, was holding a little girl with dark curly hair. She had a flowered dress on with a large ribbon that tied in the back. She was looking right at me, and I seemed to recognize her. This was my dream. I didn't think too much about it, even when I realized that I had not had a period in a while. One night I told my professor that I wasn't feeling well and that I might be getting sick. I expressed concern that I might have to leave class abruptly. It never occurred to me that I could be pregnant. I had even previously told Jay that I thought I must be heading into menopause because my periods were becoming very irregular at that point. I eventually made an appointment with a gynecologist in Virginia, since I was traveling there every week for school. The gynecologist did an exam and told me that I might be in early menopause, and she asked me if I wanted her to do some lab work, but I declined. The prospect of a potential pregnancy was far from her mind as well. Therefore, I assumed that the symptoms that I was experiencing were related to the onset of menopause.

A few more weeks passed, and I still had not had a period and I was even unsure when my last period had occurred. One day while I was at school I wondered, *Could I be pregnant?* I quickly dismissed the idea, but I couldn't forget it. I kept thinking that menopause felt a lot like pregnancy but maybe that was normal. While heading back to West Virginia from Virginia,

I stopped at a drug store in Charlottesville and bought a pregnancy test. I was embarrassed to be purchasing a pregnancy test at my advanced age of 38, so I purchased some vitamins and a protein bar and put all the items on the counter together, in one pile. Pregnancy tests had changed in the five years since Kaiden's birth. Concentrated morning urine was no longer required, so I stopped at the first rest stop on the interstate and proceeded to use it. As the stick turned blue (indicating a positive pregnancy test), I sat there for a few moments in total shock. I was not emotionally, spiritually, or physically ready to go through another pregnancy. I had not even told my husband of my suspicions. I called Jay immediately from my car phone and told him that I had just taken a pregnancy test and that it was positive. The phone went silent for a few seconds and finally he said, "I thought you were in menopause?" "I thought I was in menopause", I responded! He then said, "Bring home the test strip so I can see it," and I did. After the initial shock wore off, which took about three weeks, I told Jay about my dreams of seeing Karter holding a little dark-haired girl at my graduation. He quickly dismissed my dream. Our daughter, Kylie, was born on November 22, 1994. My pregnancy with her was uncomplicated. She was the little girl that I had seen in my dreams. God had prepared me and blessed me once again.

Pregnancy had so totally consumed my adulthood that I often overlooked the need to parent the children that I already had. Most people worry about the aging process and how they will deal with getting older. For me, my only worry about aging was that I often agonized over whether or not I would ever lose the deep desire that I had to have more and more children. My intense desire for more children finally began to dissipate as I began my walk through the darkness after Jay's secret addiction was revealed to me. This was the event that began my journey to healing this childhood wound and unlearning the lessons that my father passed down to me. I have no way of knowing the impact that my obsession to prove my worth by bearing more and more children had and will have on my beautiful children. What I do know is that my children are now a constant source of strength and hope and the affirmation that God is with me always. I have finally learned my lesson: My worth is not in my uterus but in the fact that I, too, like my children, am a precious child of God. I have faith that the lessons my children are meant to experience will be presented to them by a most tender and loving God, just as mine have been. I had to unlearn my father's lessons taught to me in childhood and recognize that my worth is limitless and has nothing to do with how many children I gave birth to. I am worthy just because I am me and I am a child of God, and there is nothing I need to do, or have, to earn that worth. I hope my story inspires all my children to recognize their own worth.

LESSON FIVE

Choosing your own life script requires courage

Life scripts are primarily shaped during the early years of childhood, centering particularly in the first seven to eight years of one's life. This life script is an unconscious life plan that is created during these formative early years in a child's life, based on their experiences as well as their interpretations of these experiences. For most people, this script acts as an imperceptible plan guiding decisions, behaviors, and even interactions throughout their life. Unfortunately, many children are often left with life scripts that do not serve their higher purpose, as they grow into adulthood, due to childhood traumas, tragedies, or even parental absences. When the life script that a child brings into adulthood no longer serves their greater good, how can a new life script be written?

The idea that I was in charge of my own destiny was always a foreign concept to me. Instead, I simply picked up the script that was handed to me by my family. My life script was shaped by my family, my church, and my hometown. I was unprepared to do anything different. I was raised in such a small world that not only were the circumstances of others lost to me, but I, too, was often lost to me. I was not raised to understand how interconnected all humans are to each other and to the universe. I was definitely raised in a patriarchal society without even knowing what that meant to me as a person or to me as a woman. As I walked outside of the tiny bubble where I was raised, I began to slowly recognize just how small my circle of knowledge had been. It was not until I was 27 years old, and had physically moved out of West Virginia, that I began to realize how diminished my understanding of the world really had been. I felt like a very small fish in a very large ocean. I had not really spent time around people who were different than me. I had not been around people of different ethnicities, races, sexual orientations, ideas, opinions, or even republicans. I was raised in a small town, as a democrat, with no real social obligation to vote or to become involved in anything outside myself. "The greater good" was a concept that I did not understand beyond the framework of my little town. I was a child, with childlike thinking, wrapped in the body of a grown woman, who also happened to be a wife and a mother. I felt a tremendous burden to figure out who I was so that I could be the parent that my children deserved me to be. However, I had no idea how or where to start.

I started imagining my life through my "Maggie mind" before I started elementary school. By the age of five, my siblings, my mother and I had all moved into a two-bedroom home with my second cousins' family. My cousins' family consisted of a mother, a father and their two sons. My family consisted of my mom, me, my older sister and two younger brothers. We had three adults and six children all under the age of eight, living in a small two-bedroom house in southern West Virginia. We had recently moved from Parkersburg to Spring Valley, West Virginia, because my dad had left us, yet again, without any means of support. This pattern of my parents' relationship always followed the same trajectory – Dad would come and live with us, mom would get pregnant, and then dad would leave. This was the pattern that I recognized as a little girl, before I was even old enough to go to school. I was never sure if my mom did not recognize this pattern of behavior or if she had just given up on trying to stabilize our childhood. I believed that she had just given up because this is about the time that my older sister, Karla, began to take over my mom's job of raising us.

My mom died on March 30, 2023, at the age of ninety-two. My two cousins from that little house came to her service and we joked about when we once all lived together in their tiny two-bedroom house. I remember the fun that we had there because they were a real family, the kind that my "Maggie mind" dreamed of having. They had two loving parents who were kind to each other and to them. This was a family that loved each other, and they opened their house and their hearts to us! They lived across the street from a creek where we spent hours and hours exploring every inch of the water and all the wildlife that lived there. I often pretended that their dad was Maggie's dad. Maggie would often blend right into this make-believe family, especially when she could not understand the events that often surrounded her own family.

I don't remember exactly how long we lived in Spring Valley, but I think it was for about one year and then my mother's parents, my Grams and Gramp, helped us rent a small house in a neighboring town, about 10 miles away. This small town is named for the place where the three states of Kentucky, Ohio, and Virginia converged before West Virginia was made into a separate state. This town would be the place that I would call my home and this was where I grew up. We moved there when I was six years old, and before my 18th birthday, we had moved five times. We moved from rental house to rental house or apartment due to our financial fragility. The town was very small. The population would peak to 5,000 in 1970 and then steadily declined to less than 3,000 in 2021.

After we moved to my hometown, my parents made one last attempt at the cycle that had defined our family. This would be the last time that my dad would come to our house in a drunken state before divorcing our mom. This would also be the conception story of my youngest brother, Knox. I was eight years old and had just started the third grade when Knox was born. I remember being at my grandmother Louise's house a few months after the event that led to Knox's conception. My dad would often stop by to see us when we were visiting with his mother. On this particular day I heard my grandmother and my dad having a stressful conversation in the living room. The tension between my dad and his mother was always unmistakable, even to me as a young child. My grandmother asked him about someone named "Joyce" and my dad stated with sternness in his voice, "She is now my W-I-F-E!" As an 8-year-old, I knew how to spell wife. I found out on that day that my dad was married to someone named Joyce! In that moment, I acted as if I did not understand their conversation but, inside I remember feeling an overwhelming sense of sadness for my mom and for my siblings. My dad had married another woman and my mom was at that time pregnant with his baby. The family cycle that defined so much of my childhood ended. My dad's marriage to Joyce broke the cycle. My grandmother Louise eventually told my mom about my dad's marriage and then eventually, we, as his children, were also told. I never told anyone about the conversation that I had overheard while visiting our grandmother Louise that day. I didn't know who I could tell.

Growing up I was often fascinated when I heard people talk about their travels, their ideas, their concerns, and their vision of a world that was so much more than I had ever imagined. Even my "Maggie mind" could not comprehend the vastness of the world that existed outside of my small hometown in West Virginia. In my first job as a nurse, a co-worker once confronted me and said that I was very judgmental and difficult to work with. Hearing her say this made me feel extremely defensive, even though it was completely accurate at that time. All these years later, I remember this one event as the first time in my life when I recognized God's grace as an attempt to pull me forward into a new way of understanding. Unfortunately, I had years of life lessons ahead of me before I could comprehend what so many took for granted as normal life skills that should have been taught and learned in my childhood.

For many years after leaving my small hometown, I could not fathom any way of thinking other than the way that I was taught. In addition to the many chapters of my life script that were written by my living and growing up in this small town in

West Virginia, I carried with me the many chapters that were added by my parents, my community, and my church. What I learned was to always stay vigil as disaster and chaos were an ever-present possibility.

The First Baptist Church was the cornerstone for everyone's morality in my hometown, including mine. At least this was my perception. Our church was the pillar of stability for me and my family. We often joked that we were at church every time the doors opened and we actually were! We went twice on Sunday, in the morning and in the evening. We also went every Wednesday night for dinner and worship service. I was in our youth choir from the time I was 12 years old until I graduated from high school. Our choir was called the New Generation Choir and it was directed by Dan Ferguson. Dan was a very successful businessman in our small town and he devoted so much of his time and energy to our choir. Every summer our choir would go on a choir tour. We went up and down the East Coast, performing concerts in local churches. Obviously, there was a cost related to these tours, and I am sorry to say that I did not pay attention to where the money for my trip ever came from, but I never missed a tour!

Prior to my mother's passing, my brother Keith and I were traveling to West Virginia to visit with her. As he drove, Keith shared a story with me from his childhood that I had not previously heard. He told me that one summer he did not have enough money to go on our upcoming choir tour and he had accepted the fact that he would not be able to go that year. At that time, he was working delivering papers each and every morning around the neighborhood and he had not yet saved enough money to cover the cost of the upcoming choir trip. He also admitted to me that during his childhood he gave almost all of his earnings to our mom to help cover the cost of our food. I was again reminded of how out of touch I was with the day to day lives of my siblings. The day before we were scheduled to leave for the choir tour, Keith was notified by our choir director that he was on the schedule to go and that his fee had been paid in full. He never knew who paid for him to go but my guess was always, Dan Ferguson. Dan was a kind and generous man. He was extremely talented as a musician and the work that he did for our church was in addition to the many businesses that he had outside of the church. He sacrificed so much for us and in looking back I hope that he knew how much he meant to me and how much the opportunity to be in the New Generation Choir stabilized my fragile existence.

My family lived on the cusp of poverty throughout my childhood and experiencing any sort of a vacation was simply out of the question. Not only were our finances very limited, but we also did not own a car until my mother remarried when I was a senior in high school. The first time that I saw an ocean was on a choir tour. My first trip to Disney World was on a choir tour. Many of the friends I made in the choir are still a significant part of my life today. I have always viewed both my church and my choir as a blessing. Many of my most cherished memories involve times spent with my friends in our church choir.

My church taught me that every girl was supposed to grow up, get married and have children. This was the unspoken lesson that I learned there. This was the best way to please God and to establish financial security. Unfortunately, getting married did not always work out like it did in my "Maggie mind." I was also taught that sinning would cause one to fall out of favor with God. I believed that the church knew of all of the sins listed in the "Sin Book." Throughout my life, I was committed to not sinning.

There were several other churches in my hometown and several more in the adjacent town. Still, as a young girl, I believed that only the First Baptist Church and the leaders of this church knew all of the answers to any of life's questions. It never occurred to me to question the authority of the church or the doctrine that they espoused as "the truth." I do remember thinking about all of my friends who attended different churches and questioning why anyone would choose another church when all the answers seemed to be available right here at ours. It was many years later when I was talking with some of my good friends from the adjacent town that I found out that their church also claimed to be the chosen church with all of the answers to life's questions. It would seem that these small churches were so focused on being "the chosen one" that they completely forgot the connection that each human has to every other living creature on this earth. Even my "Maggie mind" could not have imagined all that I now know and understand to be the truth through the grace of God.

I have struggled all my life with how I look. I have always felt an intense desire to always look pretty while carrying an extremely low level of self-confidence – this was the legacy learned from my childhood. The expectations that I had for myself were always impossible to meet. As a child, I was frail and thin. However, I started my period when I was only ten years old! Two weeks earlier than my sister, who was two years older and three grades ahead of me. Our mother did not tell us about menstruation and when it happened to me, I immediately assumed that I would be dead within days. I quickly learned to sneak my mother's Kotex pads out of her supply from our shared bathroom, to use for myself. I pinned them to my panties with safety pins since I had no other means by which to keep them on. I learned how to manage my period by watching my mom manage her own cycle. Looking back now I wish I had had the courage to ask my mom for guidance and support, but I had already learned that all I could rely on was myself.

I was the first of all of my classmates to start my period. I was only in the fourth grade. I did not know what to do with the used pads when I was at school, so I brought them home to throw away. I wrapped them in toilet paper and stuffed the used pads around the waistband of my pants. I took them home and then disposed of them in our shared family bathroom. I did not have anyone to talk to and I don't remember how long it took my mom to figure out that I was using her Kotex pads. At this point, my sister, Karla, was the main caregiver for us. Slowly, as she began to age into a teenager, she became angry and frustrated with trying to manage all of us kids. During this time, she was no longer a resource for me. This left me without anyone to talk to about my menstrual cycle. One time, while still in grade school, I went with my good friend to visit some of her relatives for a week during our summer break. My friend's family lived on a farm in a rural area of the county. Unfortunately, while I was on this trip, I started my period. My friend's family did not have indoor plumbing, which complicated an already complex situation for me. Fortunately, I had brought some Kotex pads with me in my suitcase. I begged my friend to not discuss this sensitive issue with her family, which left me to deal with the problem on my own. I made the decision to wrap up my used Kotex pads and store them in my suitcase so that I could dispose of them in private when I returned home at the end of the week. A few short weeks after I had my first menstrual cycle, Karla started her period. Over time, it became obvious to my mom that both Karla and I were having menstrual cycles. Our mom made one attempt to have a discussion with both Karla and I about this important change that was happening to our bodies. This attempt was quickly dismissed by Karla when she acknowledged to my mom that we both already knew everything that we needed to know about the topic and the discussion abruptly ended. Maybe Karla really did know everything that she needed to know about her menses, but I knew nothing, and Karla was completely unavailable to me during this time. My mom never seemed eager to parent us, so it did not take much persuading for her to abandon her efforts to inform me about anything related to puberty. During this time, I remember feeling even more alone without Karla's support available to me. I had learned to only count on myself. Because our mom had always been adamant about not sharing any family business with anyone, I made sure to only count on myself. This left my small world even smaller and there was no one around me to help me change the narrative that I had assumed to be the truth. This was written for me in the life script that I picked up from my family.

Our hometown is small, approximately 1.6 square miles. I went to C-K High School from seventh grade through 12th grade. Our hometown is separated from the neighboring town by the railroad tracks that divide our two small communities. Both towns had their own elementary schools, but the only high school was C-K High School, located on Walnut Street. When I started seventh grade, my small world expanded with the influx of students from our adjacent community. Looking back at that time, it's hard to believe that integrating students from this small town into my school seemed like such a big deal to me. But, at that time in my life, it was huge!

I spent my middle school and high school years trying to live up to my inflated standards of what it meant to be pretty. I can't say that I ever felt pretty. I was always my biggest critic. I was born with a large nose, with a bump in the middle, along with toes on each foot that were deformed. I was obsessed with my nose during those years. I often dreamed of the day when I would have the funds for rhinoplasty (a surgical procedure that reshapes the nose), but that would come much later in my life. During my high school years, Karla and I were not necessarily close, despite sharing a bedroom until she left for college. Karla was very popular and had excellent grades. I, on the other hand, struggled academically throughout middle school and high school. I was fairly popular, mostly because I was both a junior high and varsity cheerleader. I continued to struggle with low self-esteem, and I was convinced that I would forever be academically challenged. I knew that financially our family could not afford to send me to college. My dad had been willing to help pay for my sister Karla's college education because she had done so well throughout her years at school, but I knew this was not likely to be the case for me.

During my senior year of high school, I lived primarily with my dear friend, Terry. Terry was the oldest of four girls and I knew her parents as Mom and Dad. They were the normal family that my 'Maggie mind' often pretended to have. I used their station wagon to take my driver's test when I was 16 years old. I was 10 months older than Terry and I would often use her parents' car to drive her and her siblings to school whenever I was staying over, which by the time I was a senior, was pretty much fulltime.

On September 14, 2024, we had our 50th high school reunion. Initially, I had no intention of attending this event. I have a group of women who graduated from high school with me, who have been a constant source of support for me during all of these years. Of course, this group of women would be the same group that took on the planning and execution of our 50th reunion, so I had to attend. The two-day event included a meet up at the local pizza place located across the street from what used to be the high school, followed by a dinner celebration at the local country club the next day.

Since moving away from my hometown in 1983, I have only returned for brief periods to see family and friends. Other than the women in our C-K Girls group, I have not stayed connected to many others that were in my graduating class. It is a joke within our group that I remember very little about my time in high school, including the people that went to school with me.

On the first night of our high school reunion, I recognized only two people outside of the women in our C-K Girls group. On the second night, I recognized many others because the attendees were mostly the same group that had come the previous night. One of the women in our group brought a lot of pictures, yearbooks, and other C-K memorabilia for everyone to look at during the event. Terry found a document that was published by the yearbook committee as a supplement to our senior yearbook in 1974. It included answers from each senior who was asked what they hoped would happen after graduation, along with comments from the yearbook committee on what they believed would actually happen to each graduating senior. Terry had the document and she asked me if I remembered what I wrote for myself. "I'm sure it had something to do with getting married," I replied. Reading from my answer, Terry quoted my response from 1974: "I hope to be married to someone who loves me." The yearbook committee's response to my prediction for myself was "Kim will end up marrying the first person who asks her!" Hearing this had a profound impact on me that night. I grieved for that young girl whose only aspiration was to get married, as well as for all the life lessons that were headed her way.

Throughout the years we have had "C-K Girls Getaways" where we would gather someplace together for a few days to catch up and support each other. We have had the most amazing times together. These women mean the world to me and their love and support throughout the years have often carried me during the darkest times in my life, especially my dear friend, Gina. Gina was the first person that I met when I first moved to my hometown. My family had relocated from the home we shared with our cousins after the school year had already begun. When I walked into my first-grade class for the first time, Gina greeted me. She had been assigned as the class greeter for that week. Gina and I quickly became life-long friends, and we continue to consider each other as sisters! Gina is actually Jay's cousin. Gina's dad was the younger brother of Jay's paternal grandmother. When I decided to divorce Jay, I traveled to West Virginia to spend the weekend with my long-time friends, Gina and her husband, Ron. They have been some of my closest friends for many years and provided invaluable support after Jay's secrets came to light. I felt it was essential to speak with Gina in person about my decision. I will never forget her response. She said, "Kim, Jay is part of my family, but you and I are blood." That was that! Her unwavering support and love for both me and my children often served as the sole pillar of strength I could rely on during the challenging early days following the revelation of Jay's addiction.

    I met Jay when I was 20 years old. The cousin that we had lived with when I was a little girl, fixed us up on a blind date. Jay had been his best friend throughout high school. I remember being so nervous about taking a chance on a blind date, but I trusted my cousin completely! Jay was in college and had real plans for his life. I was immediately attracted to him. At that time in my life, the only way I knew to get and keep a man was to allow him to have sex with me. Jay was a virgin when we started dating and I loved that about him. He was still living at home with his parents, going to college and working part-time. I was living in my own apartment with a roommate, working full-time to support myself, and I had previously been married but was now divorced. I knew that Jay's mother did not approve of me or of her son dating me. She would often call my apartment when Jay was late getting home from our dates. All I wanted was to be deserving of Jay and his family. They did not have divorce, abortions, alcoholism, affairs, or anything bad in their family, or so I thought at that time. I carried such shame about my life and the choices that I had made. Very soon after we started dating, I fell in love with Jay, while he fell in "lust" with me. Eventually, his lust turned into love. I was over the moon when Jay told me that he loved me and wanted to marry me. I felt like I was the luckiest girl in the world. My mother enforced this truth to me on several occasions when she would tell me that Jay was the best thing that ever happened to me. Neither my mom nor I knew of God's grace.

By 1985, Jay and I were both beginning our careers. Jay was doing his residency at a Children's Hospital in Kentucky, and I was working in a local pediatrician's office as a registered nurse. Since we were both pretty settled in our careers, I decided to contact a plastic surgeon to see about having my nose "fixed." Whenever I brought up the idea of getting rhinoplasty, Jay would always tell me that I did not need to have surgery. At that time, I really believed that he loved the way that I looked and was not put off by the size of my nose. Despite his views on the matter, I continued to move forward with my mission to find a surgeon.

I asked Jay to go with me on the day that I went for my initial consult with the plastic surgeon. During the consult, I explained to the doctor what I wanted done and it was at that time that Jay immediately jumped into the conversation and said to the surgeon, "Can you do something about the bulbous tip?" Bulbous tip? I had no idea what that even meant, but during the discussion between Jay and the surgeon I came to understand that it was the tip of my nose, which Jay felt was too round and too large! I never will forget the words "bulbous tip." Finding out that Jay felt that my nose did indeed need intervention was devastating to me. My insecurities surrounding my appearance often left me feeling very vulnerable and alone. It did not take much to make my own self-doubt emerge. I convinced myself that my husband was less than thrilled about my appearance. The need to have surgery to "fix" my nose became even more important to me, after this experience.

I was scheduled for surgery two weeks later. The surgery went pretty smoothly, and I was told that my nose would remain numb for several weeks or even months following the surgery. I left the hospital with a metal splint across my entire nose. The first few days were pretty uneventful, and I continued to be so excited about the possibility of a normal sized nose! I was scheduled to go back for my first initial post-surgery checkup on Day 14. On Day 10, I had an overwhelming need to see the doctor. I was not feeling pain, per se, but still, I felt an urgency to see the surgeon immediately! I was still unable to drive because of the medication I was taking after my surgery, so I asked Jay for a ride. However, he hesitated, believing that I was simply being overly anxious.

Jay was always concerned about how his peers viewed him, and the fact that he was married to a rather emotional creature did not always sit well with him. He continued to resist my requests, so I threatened to call a taxi. Jay then begrudgingly took me to see my doctor. In the exam room, I explained to the surgeon that I felt like something was wrong underneath the metal splint. I was lying on the exam table as the doctor began to loosen the bandages from my nose and make his way down to the metal splint. The splint sat over a piece of special adhesive gauze, which stayed in place without the use of tape. My eyes were glued on the doctor's expression as he carefully removed the metal splint. Then as the gauze was pulled away from my nose, the doctor's expression turned to one of shock. Apparently, I had had an allergic reaction to the adhesive gauze underneath the splint and I now had second degree burns across my nose, which eventually required skin grafting to optimize the healing process. Despite the six-month delay in healing and a few permanent scars, I felt a sense of relief at finally having a normally sized nose.

The life script that I have inherited from my childhood contained many references to what was expected of me when I grew into an adult. From an early age I knew that I wanted to have lots of children. This was fostered by both my church and my community. It was expected that every little girl would grow up, get married and have children. For me, having children fed yet another insecurity related to my belief that since I was not smart enough to go to college and had no means to pay for college, at least I could have children!

The desire to have children was driven by the illusion that having lots of children would somehow define me and give purpose to my existence. From the time that Jay and I were married until I had my first child, I was obsessed with getting pregnant. I hoped that the deep yearning to have children would subside after I had my first child, even for a little while, but it did not. Even as I settled into being a first-time mom with my beautiful son Karter, the desire to have more children consumed me. Up until the time I had my last child at age 38, the desire was still there.

On November 30, 1995, I found out about Jay's secret life. This revelation forever changed the trajectory of my life. The desire for more children subsided and was replaced with the freshly affirmed script that "Men will always leave." My dad had left us so many times throughout my childhood that eventually, I wrote this in the life script that I picked up from my family. This belief led me down a path of multiple marriages as I allowed this belief to play out in my life over and over again. First, at the age of 18 years old, when I married a very attractive boy because I allowed him to have sex with me in the back seat of his car. This marriage ended 16 months later. I picked myself up after that marriage and entered into my second marriage with Jay just three years later.

When I married Jay, I believed with my whole open heart that this would be my forever marriage. I had a great deal to learn, but instead, this marriage ended in divorce following the revelation of Jay's secret life. After divorcing Jay, I remained single for 14 years and then hastily married a man that I was dating while I was dealing with an extreme health crisis of my youngest daughter, Kylie. It was there in the Emergency Department (ED) at Duke University, that I walked into the hall, outside my daughter's room and called Gary, the man that I was dating at that time. In that moment, the fear of losing Kylie consumed me. While talking to Gary about the events of that day, I collapsed onto the floor of the ED and cried. Gary tried to console me, but I was inconsolable. Gary and I had been dating for several months and while things seemed to going well, I couldn't honestly say that I was in love with him at that time. While I was squatted down on the floor of the ED, outside Kylie's room, Gary calmly said, "We should get married", and I agreed. Even in that moment of agreeing to get married I recognized my old patterns of wanting and desperately needing to be rescued. Recognizing this behavior was not enough; I felt powerless to do anything different.

On May 26, 2012, Gary and I got married. I remember standing in the church office with the pastor who was performing the ceremony. We were preparing to sign our legal documents and as I held the pen in my hand, I looked out the window, and could see our families in the courtyard waiting for us to come out and start the ceremony. I knew in that moment that I was making a mistake, but I did not want to disappoint our families or Gary, so I went through with it. So often, I would choose to not disappoint others, even if it meant giving up a piece of myself, instead. I rarely chose myself over others. This behavior was written in the life script that I picked up from my family.

My third husband, Gary worked out of town during the week and only came home on weekends. He owned a home in a neighboring town, which he never sold. Only a few short months after we were married, Gary moved out. I was actually relieved when it happened, but it took me a long time to convince him to sign the divorce papers. I filed for a divorce on January 7, 2014, after we had been separated for more than one year. The divorce was final on February 3, 2014, one day before my 58th birthday.

After my divorce from Gary, my children became increasingly concerned about how I was handling my relationships with men. They were concerned with my previous patterns of trusting too soon and continuing to end up alone. My marriage to Gary was especially difficult for Kylie since she was still living at home with me for the few months that Gary and I lived together. The men in my life had always found it very difficult to navigate a relationship with me because of my tight connection to all of my children, especially, Kylie.

Less than two years later, I married my current husband, Geno. At the beginning of our marriage, I pushed him away because I feared he would eventually leave, and I wanted to expedite the inevitable. He could see through my fear and he allowed me the opportunity to heal this deep wound and re-write my life script. Men do stay, but you have to pick the right person first!

November 30, 1995, the day when Jay's secret was revealed to me, occurred just a few short weeks before the end of my semester at UVA. When the new semester started in January of 1996, I made the decision to leave my infant daughter, Kylie, at home permanently, under the care of my mom. I had occasionally left her at home during my shorter school weeks, but by the time Kylie turned 14 months old, she started to miss playing with her siblings while we were in Charlottesville. On my first Monday back to school, I decided to treat myself to a massage at the hotel's spa. The spa closed at 7:30 p.m. and I was able to book the last massage of the day. It was my first trip back to school without Kylie in tow. It was also the beginning of a new semester after having only recently discovered the secret life of my husband. My spirit was so very wounded at that time. I worried that I would not be able to focus on school and continue to remain successful in my program. I was looking forward to that massage and the break it would give me from the chaos that surrounded me at that time. They booked me with a male therapist. I had been staying weekly at the same hotel for almost three years, but I had never used their spa services. My time in Charlottesville was always devoted 100 percent to school and then getting back home to my family. This massage was going to be real treat for me!

There was only one massage room, and it was positioned at the back corner of the spa area, away from the traffic of the other spa services. I met the massage therapist, who asked me a few questions about my previous massage experiences and whether there were any specific problem areas he should concentrate on during the treatment.

Everything seemed pretty standard initially, as I had had many massages throughout my life. The massage room was long and narrow. The therapist was sitting on a stool in the room and asked me to walk to the end of the room and then walk back toward him so that he could see my posture and identify any problems areas before starting the massage. I did as he requested. He then asked me to strip down to my bra and panties and do the same walk again so that he could see my body more clearly. He left the room while I took off my jeans and shirt. For a second, I had a twinge of concern about his request, but I very quickly dismissed my concerns and complied with his request. Before beginning the massage, he left the room again while I removed my bra and got on the massage table, quickly covering myself with the sheet.

The massage began with me laying on my stomach and proceeded normally. We chatted during the massage, and I shared with him that I had been coming to the hotel for almost three years. I also shared the fact that I had five children and was still nursing my youngest daughter who had recently turned one. The therapist requested that I flip over on my back and as I did, I noticed the clock on the wall. It was 7:40 p.m. and I was keenly aware that we had now gone past the 7:30 p.m. closing time of the spa. When I flipped over on my back, the therapist placed a towel across my breasts, so that he could work on my abdominal region. While this is common practice, I do remember an uneasy feeling beginning to creep up on me. I kept my eyes shut during the massage. After he completed work on my abdomen, arms, and legs, he then lifted the towel from my breasts and began massaging my breasts. I remained calm. I was determined to not change my breathing pattern as I continued to keep my eyes closed. I could feel that he was rubbing his hips up on my head and my shoulders and I could feel that he was fully aroused. Still, I remained calm.

He continued to massage my breasts. With my eyes closed, I inquired if I could go ahead and book another massage for the following Monday. He very quickly ended the massage and said, "Of course." He went on to say that he had an opening late in the evening on the following Monday around 7 p.m., that was available. I told him that would be perfect. He then said that he would step out while I got dressed. He left the room and I sat up and got dressed. After quickly dressing I opened the door to leave the spa. He met me at the door, and I continued to stay calm. I thanked him for the massage and I purposely made eye contact with him when I told him that I would see him the following week. By the time I got safely inside my hotel room, I locked my door and burst into tears. I had no idea what I should do. At that time, my relationship with Jay had become quite estranged. I decided to call my therapist. I told her what had happened and then I innocently asked her if there was any such thing as a massage for breasts. She emphatically stated, "ABSOLUTELY NOT! You were just assaulted, and you need to call the police immediately to report this incident." Feeling overwhelmed by everything, I decided to call the hotel manager instead of the police. Because I had been coming to the hotel for almost three years, the manager and I had become very close. She was a great resource for me and she had previously given me her home phone number. I called her at home and relayed all of the events of the massage. She told me to stay in my room and keep my door locked and that she would be there in 15 minutes.

As soon as she arrived in my room, I burst into tears again. After she calmed me down, she called down to the front desk and asked that one of her employees go to the spa area to make sure that it was securely locked and that all of the personnel had gone home for the night. She told her employee that she had heard some suspicious sounds coming from the spa area as she came into the hotel that night and she just wanted to make sure that everything was secured. She then turned her attention to me. Having her with me helped me see the assault for what it was. She called a friend of hers with the Charlottesville police department and within thirty minutes a female police officer arrived at my hotel room to interview me about the assault. My hotel manager friend stayed with me through the interview process with the police officer.

I had an early class the next morning and the hotel manager asked me to have all of my belongings packed up before I left the next morning for class and to leave them in the room by the door. She told me that she would call me sometime in the morning and provide me with further instructions as she did not feel that it was safe for me to return to the hotel after my classes. She said that because I had scheduled another appointment for the following week, the massage therapist would not be worried that I might tell someone about his assault.

I left for class the next morning and before leaving my room I had all of my luggage packed and sitting by the door. The hotel manager called me midmorning to tell me that she had booked me at another hotel, further out of town, under an alias name. She told me that her hotel would be covering the charges for my room until the details around the assault were worked through. After spending one night in the new hotel, I went home to North Carolina the day after my classes were finished. I had a couple of phone calls from the Charlottesville police department, and they let me know that they had arrested the massage therapist and that he was currently released on bail. The hotel manager let me know that he had been fired and that the incident had been reported to the governing board for massage therapists.

In the end, the massage therapist pled guilty and he permanently lost his massage license. I ended up dropping the criminal charges against him after his license was removed because I did not want to return to Charlottesville for the trial. A few weeks after the event occurred, I told Jay what happened with the massage therapist. The first thing that Jay said to me was, "Maybe he thought you were flirting with him when you didn't stop him when he first touched your breasts." He went on to say, "I always assumed that you were sleeping with other guys while you were away at school, anyway." He spoke to me with no emotion. I was stunned by both his response and his tone. It felt as if he had no emotional connection to me at all. At that point I knew Jay would not be able to give me the support I needed or deserved so I did not discuss the assault any further. He never asked me anything further about the incident or about how it ended. However, I did tell him that I had never even considered being unfaithful to him or to our commitment to each other.

In that moment, it became clear to me that Jay was immersed in the awareness of his own addiction and unable to see me suffering in front of him. I also recognized that I had allowed my "life spirit" to become depleted. I was surviving but not living in my full, aware state of being. After this event, I made some drastic changes in my life. I knew that I needed to surround myself with support to help me through the dark space

I was currently moving through. I had previously seen a massage therapist, Lynn, who worked at a local spa in my hometown. She had massaged me a few times and I contacted her about another massage. When we got together, I told her about the events surrounding the assault. I learned that Lynn was a spiritual healer as well as a massage therapist. I made plans to meet with her at her home that same week. Over the next few months, Lynn and her sister became the support that I needed in my life. They held the light for me on my own spiritual journey until I was strong enough to hold the light for myself. Today, I can recognize that Lynn's support saved my life over those next months as I prepared to walk out of the darkness that I was living in at that time, with Jay. I was a novice when it came to writing my own life script, but events such as these provided me with the courage to recognize that I could re-write my own life script!

I still had more to learn about re-writing my story. The opportunity to go to college was something that I assumed would never be given to me. With the help and support of Jay, I learned how to navigate the many processes involved in applying for and seeking higher education. More importantly, he encouraged me through my early years of college, until I had the confidence to help myself. Each of the four degrees that I have earned gave me the strength and determination to keep going forward. The end for me was earning my doctorate degree. Because my doctorate degree took me seven and a half years to complete, it spanned across a time in my life when I would experience an immense life change that could have easily interrupted or even halted my ability to complete that last degree. Once I started working on this degree, I would constantly hear the words of my mother when I was a little girl telling her story to others about how she would have finished college and become a teacher if it weren't for all of her children keeping her from fulfilling her dreams. This made me even more determined to write my own life script, because I wanted to demonstrate to my children that I was important to me, and this meant that they were important to me.

Still, I often hesitated to put myself first, even when it came to something that was important to me, like my doctorate degree. My program was a 7-year program, meaning that each student was required to complete the program within this timeframe. Unfortunately, it took me 7 and a half years to finish my program due to the delays that I encountered during my pregnancy with Kylie while in my 2nd year. Most doctoral programs are set up very similarly: the first two to three years are devoted to classroom course work, followed by the completion of a grant proposal that would be ready for submission to a funding source before moving on to the final phase of the program – the dissertation. Essentially, the grant proposal would outline the first three chapters of the dissertation process. A dissertation is a comprehensive, original research project that is undertaken by doctoral candidates, which serves as the culmination of their academic studies. It is intended to contribute to the scientific knowledge of a specific academic field and serves as evidence of the candidate's expertise. Dissertations are made up of five chapters: Chapter 1 is the introduction to the problem, Chapter 2 is a comprehensive review of the current relevant published research, Chapter 3 is the methodology which outlines the process for conducting the proposed research project, Chapter 4 is the results section that outlines the results of the project, and in Chapter 5, there is a discussion of the results focusing on the relevance of the results against the currently published literature. The grant proposal would serve as a template for my upcoming research project that I, as a doctoral student, had to complete in order to fulfill the requirements for a PhD.

The long commute to and from UVA, coupled with my work and family obligations left me far behind with my own grant proposal. I was, of course, working against a rigorous timeline that was set by the university. Suddenly, I was left with only one month to complete my grant proposal. During this time, the stress between Jay and I seemed palpable. It seemed that every time I was able to block out some time to work on my grant, Jay would be unable to help me by taking care of the children or helping with the other household obligations that often occur when you have a lot of children. One afternoon, I talked Jay into taking the kids to the park without me. I had made the decision that I was going to leave for a few days in order to get my grant completed. At that moment, I felt that sharing my plans with Jay would somehow impede my progress on my grant. After he left with the kids, I quickly packed up a small suitcase along with all of the documents that I needed to complete my proposal. During the previous week, I had spent an extra day at the university library collecting and copying all of the relevant research documents that I would need to complete my grant assignment.

 I got in my car and drove to the park. I did not want the kids to see me because I knew that my youngest daughter, Kylie, would want to stay with me. Luckily, the parking lot for the park was located near the entrance and I was able to slip in beside Jay's car and place a note on his seat before leaving. In my note, I told Jay that I needed to get away for a few days so that I could complete the work on my grant. I told him that I would call him and let him know where I was when I had found someplace to stay. At that point, I had no idea where I was going but I was planning on heading toward Asheville, North Carolina. Eventually, as I was traveling, I saw a sign for the Grove Park Inn, and I immediately pulled over to call the number on the sign. It was around 1998 and even though I had a car phone, it was not a smart phone by any stretch of the imagination! The car needed to be sitting still and in a place with good reception, which was often difficult to find in the mountains of North Carolina. After making the call, I was able to get a room at the Grove Park Inn, so I headed toward the resort.

Grove Park Inn is a historic resort hotel in Asheville, North Carolina, that offered incredible views of the Blue Ridge Mountains. As a family, we had previously visited the Grove Park and even though I knew it was expensive, I decided to go there to stay. I was determined to finish my grant and move to the last phase in my doctoral education. At that point in my life, I was beginning to feel like Jay was actually sabotaging my chances of finishing my degree. I have no idea if I was just feeling overwhelmed and sorry for myself or if in some way, he actually wanted me to fail. Regardless of the truth, these feelings made me push myself even harder to accomplish my goal! After arriving at the Grove Park, I called and left a message at home so that Jay would know where I was in case of an emergency. My mom was still making the trip from West Virginia to North Carolina to watch our children through the week. I knew that she would be at my house to help Jay with the kids while I was gone, even if Jay got called into the hospital, which, of course, was inevitable.

I stayed at the Grove Park for seven days and six nights. Once I had checked into my room, I did not leave the room until I was ready for checkout! I ordered room service twice a day and I worked 10 to 12 hours a day on my grant proposal. I would occasionally take a break and sit in my windowsill overlooking the mountains, enjoying the beautiful scenery, then I would immediately return to working on my grant. It took me almost a week, but I finished my grant proposal and headed back home. I don't really remember Jay's reaction to my disappearance, but I felt so accomplished to have completed my project on time. By this time in our marriage, our relationship had become very strained. Jay was struggling with his own recovery and the support that we had previously given to each other no longer existed. For me, I was focused entirely on finishing my degree and attempting to meet the needs of all of my children. I can honestly say, without hesitation, that I was less focused on my kids and more focused on finishing school. It wasn't long after this event that my marriage ended for good, and Jay moved out of our home for the last time.

Several weeks after my grant proposal was accepted by my institution, I was officially notified by the university that I had been moved to the final phase of my doctoral degree: the dissertation phase. This was a real accomplishment for me and for the first time since starting on this degree in 1993, I finally had no doubt that I would be able to complete my degree. One day I went by Jay's office to talk with him about one of our children. After we had finished our discussion, I got up to leave and Jay stood up and looked at me in a way that made me remember why I loved him. "Congratulations on finishing your grant," he said, quietly. At first, I felt shocked that he was even aware that my grant had been accepted, but I knew that he was talking regularly to our children, and I assumed that one of them had told him. Regardless, when he said this to me, I was immediately consumed with sadness at the thought that we were no longer together. When it came to Jay, my strength and focus fluctuated like the wind rustling through the trees. One minute I believed strongly that I was going to finish my degree and be able to take care of my children and then in the next, I would be consumed with loneliness and self-doubt that I could successfully take care of myself and our children without Jay in my life. I thanked him and as I reached for his office door handle, he handed me a card. After I got inside my car, I opened it immediately. The card read: "I knew you could do it! I am very proud of you. Love, Jay." I knew that he meant what he had written in that card, despite all that had transpired between us. Jay's authentic self was still there, often too deep inside him for me to see. I missed him terribly, but I had to let him go.

Learning to write my own life script was difficult. As long as I can remember, my mind has frequently vacillated between good thoughts and negative thoughts. This thought pattern presented itself as whispers of self-doubt which culminated in the illusion that I was unworthy. For a long time, I recognized these negative tapes that seem to play over and over in my head as something that I carried forward from my childhood into adulthood. It took me a long time to not only acknowledge their presence, but to understand the patterns they form and the triggers in me that summon them. The process of releasing them required a blend of compassion, commitment and the courage to let them go. Over-time, the freedom from negative self-chatter allowed me the opportunity to understand their origin and then choose to no longer nurture their presence in my life.

The life script handed to me by my parents, my upbringing, my community, and my church did not serve me. Over the years, I had become obsessed with reading any and all self-help books that I could find. Great books by Carolyn Myss, *The Creation of Health*, *Anatomy of the Spirit*, *Why People Don't Heal and How They Can*, books by Don Miguel Ruiz, including *The Four Agreements*, and Gary Zukav's, *Seat of the Soul*. These books began to awaken something inside of me that was separate from my past. It was a connection to something larger than my history and deeper than my understanding. Slowly I was becoming courageous; at times, I was fearless. I recognized that I had the courage that I needed to write my own life script. Accepting yourself as courageous can at times be very scary, but I believe that it is the single most important ingredient to be able to write your own life script. Be brave!

LESSON SIX

Learn to forgive imperfect parenting

All of my children have encountered difficulties as a result of the choices I've made throughout my life, including my struggle with an eating disorder and my choice to move them far away from their father. Additionally, there were many other decisions I made along the way that lacked the foresight to consider how they would impact my children. Watching my children suffer because of my actions has been challenging, and learning to forgive myself for those decisions has proven to be just as difficult. My youngest child,

Kylie, was just four years old in 1999 when I moved myself and my five children 600 miles away from their father after our divorce had finalized. At that time, I believed I was making the only decision I was capable of making.

After relocating to Memphis, I took Kylie and Kaiden to visit their father about once a month. When we first moved, my two oldest children were preparing to start college. They both enrolled at the University of Memphis, but early on, they decided together to return to North Carolina for their college educations. Meanwhile, my middle son, Karson, was in high school. My older children made their own arrangements to see their dad, often opting to visit him on their own schedule, separate from the younger kids. I have limited insight into how Kylie and Kaiden's visits with their dad went, but I do know that Kylie experienced significant changes during this time. She began exhibiting extreme behavioral shifts, often coming home from her visits feeling sick to her stomach and frequently vomiting throughout her first night back. I began to understand from Kaiden that Kylie consumed a lot of sugar and soda during their visits with their dad. This was typically not part of her diet when she was home. I also learned that Kylie appeared very stressed during these visits. Once, when Kylie was around six years old, she returned home after visiting her dad and asked me if I could help him get a divorce, as she thought he was unhappy and that his new wife was unkind to him. I tried to gently explain to her that her dad was an adult and capable of taking care of himself. Gradually, Kylie began to harbor resentment toward her dad's new wife, seeming to blame her for all the pain she was experiencing in her life. The truth for Kylie was that she missed her dad and felt overwhelmed by the emotions stemming from the numerous changes that had occurred in her young life. Many of Kylie's feelings were displaced onto her dad's wife because she needed someone to blame for the experiences that she was having at that time. She was just a little girl. Even though she was in therapy during this time, the absence of her dad in her everyday life became the void that she would spend most of her young life trying to fill.

The textbook reaction for young girls to the "absent father" is to try and fill the emptiness through other relationships. During her teenage years, Kylie kept trying to find someone to make her feel okay about herself. Unfortunately, she was constantly picking partners who were also trying to fill their own voids. As a mother it is hard to watch your child be hurt over and over again. Of course, I knew she played a role in her own pain. Choosing people for the wrong reasons brings forth a lesson that must be addressed; otherwise, it will recur repeatedly. This gives the individual an opportunity to recognize the lesson and heal a wound. As a mother I felt an overwhelming desire to protect her from herself, but I had to often remind myself that if I took away her lesson, I would be taking away the gift that she would receive when her lesson was both recognized and dealt with. I reminded myself of this fact, over and over again.

After dealing with epilepsy, craniofacial surgery to correct a congenital birth defect, and many other "close calls," Kylie was forced to face her decisions about needing and using relationships to define herself. At 20 years old, she went through many life-changing decisions that would impact the rest of her adult life. As hard as it was, I had to let her go. I could not make this go away for her. I could not make her learn the lessons that were being presented to her. God held me tight as he slowly pried her from my grip and I let go of her, knowing that she was in God's hands. My prayer was that she, too, would soon realize that she was safe in God's hands and she would be led where she needed to go.

The lessons that I have been presented with in my life have at times knocked me to my knees and forced me to go in directions that I would not have otherwise gone. However, watching my baby girl struggle to find her "father's love" over and over again, all the while looking in the wrong places, broke me open. In the book *Broken Open* by Elizabeth Lesser, the author talks about times in our lives when our life experiences cause us such immense pain that we are literally broken open and forced to make a change. I often wanted to resist the truth that I could not protect her anymore – I would have given my life to make her life somehow easier or less painful. My resistance of this truth caused me to shut people out of my life and retreat into myself. There were times when I felt such deep depression that it often consumed me.

Depression has taken over my life many times. There were days when I struggled to put one foot in front of the other. My childhood had taught me that I could only count on myself, thereby teaching me to not reach out for support from others. Instead, I would "circle my wagons" for a long fight. I often feared that I would not make it out alive, but so far, I have continued to have the opportunity and the strength to face one lesson after another. At the end of the day, I have found that no matter what is going on in my life, my lesson is to stay calm in each and every storm. I've had to remind myself that I have my lessons, and Kylie must learn hers – on her own.

I was often overwhelmed with Kylie and all the "situations" that she often found herself in. Every parent knows that when you first find out that your child has become sexually active, it changes the way that you see them. Gone was the little girl who seemed so very innocent. Gone was the young girl that I could protect and shelter from life's biggest obstacles – relationships! Often, I have wished that I could have been a better role model for her.

Unfortunately, Kylie had the mother that she had. She had a mother who stayed single for more than 14 years after divorcing her father and then hastily married a man that she should not have married. I struggled for two years to try and understand why I married again, after divorcing Jay. Eventually, I came to understand that I agreed to marry a man because I wanted to be rescued from the pain and isolation that I found myself in at that point in my life. I was so tired. I was tired of being alone and having to deal with Kylie and her physical health. I simply needed someone to scoop me up, hold me in their arms and tell me that she was going to be okay and that I no longer had to prepare myself that she might die before me.

It took me a long time to admit that out loud. My biggest fear was that Kylie would die young and I would somehow be expected to live in this world without her. I have said these words only to my therapist and to two of my closest friends. The powerlessness that I felt around Kylie's health is and always was palpable. Even now, I have to remind myself over and over again that I am not alone, because when it comes to Kylie's health, I feel all alone. Normal teenage behavior is much more serious when they have epilepsy. I can still feel that "fight or flight" response every time I hear a loud noise. I know what it is like to hear your child drop hard on the floor, knowing that she has had another seizure. I try to stay calm, but my body reacts with the memory of finding her on the floor convulsing in a grand mal seizure. I wish I could lose that cellular memory of her seizures but even now my reaction to her seizures is still very raw. Memories, both good and bad, serve a purpose in our life. They allow us the opportunity to think back to a previous similar experience when we reacted differently. The cumulative effect of remembering allows us the opportunity to grow in ways that we may have previously been unable to do. With Kylie, I struggled to react differently, but I knew I had to keep trying.

My first son came to me in a quiet celebration of my "Life Plan," just as I had planned it. I was 25 years old. I had planned my life with the naïve mind of a girl who had so much to learn and who thought that this life plan was the same for everyone — get married, have children, live a happy life. I held on to this dream, even though my first marriage was at the age of 18, to a man who beat me up weekly, and that marriage ended 16 months later in a divorce and with an abortion.

Still, I held fast to the dream. So, when I married for the second time, I was ready to implement the Life Plan. After three years of trying, I finally got pregnant. The pregnancy was difficult, long and kept me numb with fear. Still my life plan was in motion. My first son was the perfect child, he hit every milestone at the perfect time, acted in a perfect way and thus confirmed my belief that having the Life Plan meant that it would always be followed. Karter was an easy child. He made me believe that motherhood was a job for which I could and would succeed. Karter was both quiet and polite. He was a good sleeper and required little, if any, discipline. He was a people pleaser, even to his parents. He never wanted us to be upset or disappointed with him. He was an absolute joy to parent and in many ways, I know that I have failed him the most because I believed in a false reality that it was my skillset as a parent that molded this perfect little boy. The reality was that he came to me this way.

As Karter grew up, I saw glimpses of the anxiety that would reside in him for many years. There was one particular time when Karter was in the third grade that I saw how much his anxiety and fear directed and consumed his young life. I had been very sick after an ectopic pregnancy (a pregnancy in which a fertilized egg implants and grows outside of the uterus which requires immediate surgical intervention) had ruptured and I required hospitalization for a couple of weeks. Not long after that event I found out that I was pregnant with my third son, Kaiden. The pregnancy with Kaiden was very difficult and Karter began having a difficult time separating from me in order to go to school. It got so bad one day that he refused to go into his classroom, which was entirely out of character for him. On this particular day he was screaming and crying with both of his little arms wrapped around my waist, begging me not to leave him. I pried his arms from around my waist and as his teacher held him in place, I walked through the doorway and the door between us, closed. I left him at school when he was begging me to stay. I so regret that day. I did not understand what was wrong. I did not see how scared he was that he might come home and perhaps find both me and his unborn brother in the hospital, yet again. I did very little explaining back then. Even though I tried to explain as much as I could, I was still working under the expectation that life should go on as normal and that my children would be unaffected by the grief that was often consuming me. Karter needed me and I was not there – neither physically nor emotionally. I know that this event had a profound impact on Karter, and I also understand, now, that Karter was teaching me how to be a better mother.

When the time came to have another child, after Karter's birth, the life plan that I had put into place when I married Jay did not hold the true. My second and third pregnancies ended with miscarriages. Three years after my first son was born, I welcomed my second son, Karson. Karson came into the world quietly but exploded into a fury of activity. Karson was an active, wildly curious, child. He knew no fear and it became a full-time job just to keep him safe. Karson challenged me on every front at every opportunity with every moment of every day. I knew from the time that Karson was an infant that there was a light that existed in him that not only attracted people to him but also, on a deeper level, I knew that this child was not going to be as easy as my first son! I was definitely not prepared to parent such a bright, wild and fearless child.

When Karson was a toddler, I placed calls to the poison control center three times for three separate events! I was concerned that the Department of Social Services (DSS) might take him from my custody, believing that I wasn't providing the protection he needed. Despite my desires and attempts to keep him from getting into things, Karson found anything and everything that he could and he put them in his mouth. Over about an 18-month period, he drank half a bottle of Triaminic, one third of a bottle of liquid Tylenol, and he drank a few swallows of hydrogen peroxide. Each time, I would call the number for poison control, they would instruct me on what to do and what I needed to look out for in case he needed to be taken to the nearest hospital. Karson was about two years old when he drank the liquid Tylenol. I was instructed by poison control that I needed to keep him awake as long as possible and that he should not be left alone. For about the next three hours, Karson ran around the house like a wild animal, which was not that different from his usual behavior. I was so scared. I was home alone with my two sons. Karter was about five years old and he stayed right by my side the entire time. I tried to get Karter to go on to bed but he would not leave Karson or me. We both followed Karson everywhere he went. After a few hours of hyperactivity, Karson stood in the hallway outside his bedroom, jumping up and down while swinging his security blanket against the wall for what seemed like hours. Finally, after several more hours, Karson fell asleep on the floor, with his blanket. I called poison control back and gave them an update and they told me he should be fine and to let him sleep through the night. I carried him to bed. Karter had stayed with him through that entire ordeal. Karter was always thinking of everyone else, even though he was himself, a little boy.

A few months later, while visiting my mom in West Virginia, I had to make another call to poison control. I had just given a bath to Karter and Karson, and they were both in their pajamas when I left them upstairs to play while I went downstairs to get them both some water to drink before putting them to bed. While I was getting their cups filled with water, Karter came downstairs while I was in the kitchen. I quickly realized that Karson was upstairs alone. I went to the bottom of the stairs and called for Karson to come downstairs. I could hear the soles of his footie pajamas as he walked on the carpet toward the stairway. As he got to the top of the stairs, I could see that look on his face – the look that tells me that he has been into something that he shouldn't have been. I said, "Karson did you get into something in Nana's bathroom"? He opened his mouth to respond and out came bubbles! I ran up the stairs and scooped him into my arms as I headed towards the bathroom. On the floor was an opened bottle of hydrogen peroxide. I tried to make him spit into the sink, but he didn't know how to spit. I ran downstairs and gave him some water to drink while I called poison control. Poison control assured me that small amounts of hydrogen peroxide in a toddler would have little to no side effects other than, perhaps, an upset stomach. I was so relieved. I remember the look on Karter's face when he realized that he had inadvertently left Karson, unattended, upstairs and I knew that he was feeling responsible. I assured Karter that Karson knew better than to get into the cabinet under the bathroom sink. Karter was relieved that Karson was not in any danger from drinking the hydrogen peroxide. Karson made it through each potential poison event, but I quickly realized that Karson was fearless, and helping him establish boundaries as he grew older was going to be a necessity. Karter took on a lot of responsibility as a child because I counted on his help. I recognize that I should not have depended so much on a child's help and as his mother I should have known better. Most of my memories with my children do not include my husband. Jay was often very busy at the hospital and as time passed, he became even more removed from our family. His busy practice coupled with his own internal struggles kept him isolated, away from our family. I admit that I depended on Karter too often and too soon. Most of his childhood was taken up with the task of watching over the other kids. He was an amazing big brother, but I regret not allowing him time to have a longer childhood before he stepped into that role.

I met our "soon to be" oldest daughter, Mona, when we moved in next door to her and her biological family. Mona was nine years old. She was standing at the fence that divided our two properties, talking to Karter and Karson. She was such a curious little girl, with dark curly hair. It did not take long for her to become Karter and Karson's best friend. Mona was at our house or Karter and Karson were over at her house almost all of the time. I referred to them as The Three Musketeers! When they were home from school they were rarely apart. Many times, on the weekend, they would all three camp out in our treehouse in our back yard. They had fixed up the treehouse by painting the inside and placing mattresses on the floor for everyone to sleep on. They had even figured out a way to hook up their video games on a small television by running a long extension cord in through the garage window. One time they actually ordered a pizza to be delivered to their tree house! The Musketeers were inseparable. I accepted this as fact and when I had to hire a babysitter to watch the kids during the summer months, Mona was included as one of my kids.

Each and every babysitter I found ended up staying only briefly. The Musketeers proved to be quite a handful and they, collectively, saw each babysitter as a challenge. From sitting in a tree shooting their water guns at unsuspecting people driving by with their windows down to having then seven-year-old Karson read out loud to the babysitter excerpts from the book *What's Happening to my Body – Book for Boys*, the Musketeers were a force that always proved too much for any babysitter. Eventually, I gave up trying to find a sitter and Karter and Mona were tasked with the role of watching over Karson and Kaiden while I was working.

Jay was never satisfied to stay too long in any city and our move to the mountains in the southern part of West Virginia was no exception. So, in the summer of 1994, we got ready to move again. None of us were prepared to leave Mona behind. The Musketeers approached me about having a talk with Mona's biological mom about the possibility of her moving with us to North Carolina. I know how unusual that sounds but it is difficult to explain the connection that we had to Mona and that she had with us. At that time, Mona's parents were going through a very difficult divorce and within a very short amount of time it was decided that both Mona and her biological mom would move with us to North Carolina. It was just meant to be! The divorce was very hard on Mona. In her mind, she and her biological father were very close, as she was the youngest of the three children. At the time of the divorce, the two older children were away at separate boarding schools. I know that Mona was as drawn to all of us as we were to her. The security of our family was exactly what Mona needed during this time in her life and Mona was exactly what we needed to complete our family. Initially, Mona split her time between our house and living with her biological mother. Then, eventually she came to live with us full time and we accepted her as our own and she accepted us as her own.

Despite having many miscarriages during the early years of my marriage to Jay, my desire for children was a driving force inside of me. I never took into account how my miscarriages impacted the children that I already had or even whether or not it was wise for me to keep trying to get pregnant again and again. I often thought about whether my health, my eating disorder, or the fact that I had experienced a ruptured ectopic pregnancy less than two months before getting pregnant with Kaiden, impacted my subsequent pregnancy with him. Were the problems in Kaiden's pregnancy caused by the decisions that I had made previously? Even now, I don't have any answer to these questions. However, I do recognize that my desire for more children had a profound impact on all of my children. For a long time, I failed to acknowledge the risks I had come to accept as normal while striving for a successful pregnancy.

As an infant, Kaiden was extremely fussy. Even saying that he was fussy is such an understatement. The medication that I had taken for several months to keep him from going into heart failure before his birth, resulted in his central nervous system becoming hyper-stimulated. This was the rationale that we received after countless doctor's appointments to try and figure out if he was in pain or if he was suffering in any way. He was difficult to breastfeed because he could not be soothed or settled in any way. His sleep patterns were very brief, at best, and parenting such a fussy infant after a very long and difficult pregnancy was extremely challenging. Kaiden continued to miss milestone after milestone and eventually we were told that he was most likely autistic, even though this diagnosis could not be determined until the age of two. After months of agony, the decision was made to try and give him a mild sedative, to help lessen the sensitivity of his central nervous system. He spent so much time crying that he had been unable to gain the appropriate weight and had by then fallen off the standardized growth chart. The standardized growth chart is used to plot measurements like weight, length, and head circumference against the age of the child to help ensure that children are on track with their growth and development. Falling off the growth chart is a real call to action for any healthcare provider and parent. At that time, most of the calories that Kaiden was consuming were being used to sustain his hyper stimulation. Months passed without relief, and I grieved for my beautiful boy who seemed to be in a constant state of panic or pain. Jay and I spent countless hours tag teaming Kaiden's care while still trying to parent our two oldest sons. All I can remember during that first year of Kaiden's life was complete and utter exhaustion. As soon as Jay would come home from work, he would take over the care of Kaiden so that I could rest and recuperate in preparation for the time when Jay would need to return to work. I have very few memories of my two oldest sons during this time. I know this had to be a stressful time for them as well.

After starting Kaiden on the medication, his behavior and demeanor changed. He became calmer, he started to put on some weight and he also seemed to be making more eye contact with us. We were unsure what had caused the changed in his behavior. Was it the sedatives that allowed his central nervous system to calm down? Perhaps it was the passage of time or the fact that eventually he had processed all of the medication from his system that I had taken during the pregnancy. Whatever the reason, his behavior improved. However, he was still missing milestones and at 12 months of age, he was not sitting up without support, much less standing or walking. We had an appointment scheduled with a specialist in Memphis at around 18 months of age. As we waited for the day of the appointment to arrive, Jay and I both worried about the outcomes of the consultation, but we were determined to give Kaiden every opportunity that we possibly could. Approximately two weeks before our scheduled consultation, Kaiden started sitting up by himself, crawling and, a week later, he took his first steps! Our Kaiden had defied the odds, yet again. By the time he was 18 months old he had caught up with all of his milestones, and we cancelled our appointment with the specialist in Memphis.

In 1999, as my divorce from Jay continued to proceed through the court system, I made plans to move my children and myself from North Carolina to Memphis, Tennessee. This decision was months in the making. At that time, I was in constant contact with my brother, Knox, who had helped me secure a realtor in Memphis so that I could purchase a home for our family. I was continuing to work with my therapist who at that time lived in Florida, along with my spiritual teacher who lived in Hickory, close to where we were currently living. This team surrounded me with the support that I needed to make one of the biggest decisions that I had ever made for my family. Looking back, I don't know why I felt like I had to keep my decision to move to Tennessee a secret from my younger children, but I did. I felt paralyzed with fear that Jay would somehow stop me from moving us to Memphis and try and take our children away from me. The possibility that I might lose my children was the fear that drove so many of my decisions at that time. Jay and I had already completed the mediation process with the court system, and I had been granted full custody of the children, but still my fear felt valid. Making decisions from a place of fear set the stage for poor decision-making on my part. Karter and Mona both knew that we would be leaving in April, and they would be staying in North Carolina until they both completed their senior year of high school. Then they would join us in Memphis, together, after graduation. On the Thursday before we were scheduled to move, I told both Kaiden and Karson that we would be moving to Memphis the following day. Kylie was only four years old, and I had Karter take her to our local McDonalds so that she could play on the playground while

I talked to her brothers about our upcoming move. I remember very little of that conversation. I know that it took place, but I have no memory of their responses. I am sure they were both shocked, even traumatized by the reality of our upcoming move, but I continued to move forward.

I admit that at that time in my life I was so traumatized myself that I felt like I was in survival mode. All I could think about in that moment was getting the moving truck packed and then getting my three youngest children in the car and heading to Memphis, Tennessee. The only memory that I have of moving day was the exact moment that we crossed the North Carolina border into Tennessee. I remember feeling such an enormous sense of relief – relief that I had pulled it off, we had moved out of North Carolina, without Jay knowing. Every day in our new house I anticipated that Jay was going to call me and confront me about having moved, but that never happened. Seven days after we moved to Memphis, I got a call from Jay, asking about seeing the kids, and I told him that we had moved the previous week to Memphis. I held my breath in anticipation of his response and then he calmly said, "Oh, you moved?" That was it! There was no shocking response or retribution. He seemed so matter of fact that his response felt like another jab to my already broken heart.

When Karson was in the nineth grade, he wrote a poem for one of his classes titled "Moving Day Happened Anyway." In the poem he talked about how hard it was for him to leave his school and his friends in North Carolina and move to Memphis and to a new school. His poem was submitted by his nineth grade teacher to the Young Writers USA (a national writing contest organization that offers contests for schools and students) and was later published in their annual book of winning poems. I know that my decision to move us to Memphis had a profound impact on Karson. As an adult he has shared with me about the many struggles that he faced because of the move. All of my children have shared with me how this move negatively impacted their subsequent relationship with their dad. Kylie was only four years old when we moved. She has expressed to me that the move to Memphis made it harder for her to have a close relationship with her dad.

There is no pain that is more difficult for a parent than watching your child suffer. I have heard people say that hindsight is always 20/20 and without a doubt this is so true. The reality that some of my decisions caused pain and suffering for my children was slow to emerge for me. This is a difficult reality to accept for any parent. When your primary role as a parent is to protect your children, it is uncomprehensible to believe that because of me and my decisions, my children suffered. I have come to understand and even forgive my younger self for decisions made without understanding the implications of those decisions on my children. I have at times even asked for forgiveness from my kids for many of the decisions that I have made, which negatively impacted their lives.

Despite the hurt and pain that I have unwittingly caused them, the love that my kids and I have for each other is matched only by the immense bond that exists between all five of my children. For me as a mom, seeing the relationship that exists between my children is the most magical part of being their mom. Despite all that my children have experienced, often due to the decisions that I have made without the consideration or understanding of the implications of those decisions, they remain connected to each other in such a beautiful way.

LESSON SEVEN

Addiction is an opportunity for change

Addiction is one of those words that conjures up many different interpretations depending on the individual. For me, the definition of addiction is anything that causes someone to have a compulsive need to only want to do one thing. When someone only wants to do one thing, then the rest of their life and everyone in that life remain out of balance. My understanding of my addiction becomes even more complicated because I believe that, in many ways, it has at times saved my life. Over the course of my life, I have found that, like so many things, addiction has both a light and dark side – a good side and a shadow side. And both can serve as an opportunity and as a teacher, for change.

When I was a young child, I watched my mom sitting in the dark eating a bag of chips, thinking that it was her secret. I also remember watching my grandfather – her father – sitting in the dark eating, alone, again thinking that no one knew his secret. They were both trying to deal with their uncomfortable feelings by eating. As a child, I was keenly aware of everything around me. Even though I had little comprehension of the chaos that constantly surrounded us as a family, still I watched. In those moments of watching, I decided that I would never be fat. Neither my mom nor my grandfather would be classified as fat, but to me, they were fat. I have no idea where my metric for measuring fatness originated, but in my "Maggie mind," the metrics were my mom and my grandfather. My mother's mother, we called her Grams, weighed 112 pounds all of my life. She was very vocal about her weight and she would often tell me what she weighed. Grams was very focused on her outward appearance. She was a first-grade teacher for many years and was always impeccably dressed. She picked out her clothes, shoes, and hosiery each night before going to bed. When I was young, I can remember seeing her clothes hanging on the hook of her closet door. Her shoes were positioned beside her closet door with her hosiery folded neatly on top. The first thing she did every morning was to weigh herself and then she would get fully dressed for the day ahead. Even years after she had retired, this remained her daily ritual. Her hair was always perfect and her makeup flawlessly applied. This ritual continued every day of her life until she was eventually placed in a long-term care facility near the end of her life, well into her late 90s. My Grams was very important to me. She often told me that I was her favorite grandchild. I never heard these words from anyone else in my life, so these were words that nurtured my soul when I was a little girl. I thought of my Grams as someone who had it all – looks and money! For me that was all that anyone could aspire to achieve.

My grandparents lived and worked most of my life in Clearwater, Florida. My grandfather served as a principal for several different school systems throughout his career. They would return to West Virginia during the summer months and then return to Florida in time for the start of the new school year. While my Grams was in West Virginia, she always made an appointment to go the "Smart Shop," and she usually took me with her. The "Smart Shop" was a specialty store in downtown Huntington, which featured professional business wear for women. My Grams knew someone who worked at the dress shop who saved special outfits throughout the winter months that were both stylish and sized to fit my Grams. We would go there for our annual visit, and I would sit on the small stage in front of three large, curved mirrors that surrounded the platform. My Grams would try on outfit after outfit and each time she would walk down to the platform to review her reflection. I was mesmerized by every outfit. The salesperson always completed each outfit with the perfect shoes, bag, gloves, and hat, if needed. We would spend the whole afternoon like this, with me sitting there watching her try on every outfit. Before we ended the day, Grams would make a large purchase of all her favorite items. I have no memory of how much she spent each summer at the "Smart Shop," but to me, money was never a worry for her. In my "Maggie mind," I wanted to grow up and never have to worry about money, but I had no idea how that could ever be a reality for me.

Having my grandparents return to West Virginia each summer was always a huge treat for me as a child. My grandparents had three daughters and they all lived very close to each other in West Virginia, which made spending time with my cousins very convenient. As a child, I assumed that my grandparents' life in Florida consisted entirely of work. In 2024, my siblings and I met in Asheville, North Carolina, to celebrate the life and recent passings of our mother and our precious brother, Kris. Kris's beloved daughter, Kayla and his treasured grandson, Jason, joined us for that weekend. My sister brought a huge box of old slides that belonged to both my grandparents and to my mother. She also brought along an old slide projector, and we spent one entire evening looking through the old slides that most of us had never seen before. These slides revealed the real life that my grandparents had in Florida, which was a total surprise to all of us. Apparently, my grandparents spent a lot of time boating, bowling, and eating out with a large group of friends. They looked like they were having the time of their lives and it was such a treat to see them enjoying their life and each other to the very fullest! The slides turned out to be such a gift for all of us.

My Grams had a huge impact on my life as a child and in many ways her perception about her appearance had a profound impact on my own life, as I grew up. I was always focused on my appearance and I was always my biggest critic when it came to how I looked. There were a lot of times when being thin was the most important thing to me. I can recall from a very early age having many aversions to different foods, including textures, tastes and smells. I knew from an early age that I did not want to eat any animal protein. Eventually, by the time I was 19, I was a complete vegetarian. Being a vegetarian was, at times, a pretense to cover up my anorexia. While it was true that eating animal protein disgusted me, eating much of anything in those early years disgusted me. It was easier to say that I was a vegetarian rather than anorexic and at that time I really did not understand that my relationship with food was an addiction. I had been primed since infancy to focus on my appearance, and food was my solution. It took me a long time to unpack my relationship with food and really understand exactly what it meant to me and how it had impacted those in my life.

My dad used to tell the same story over and over of when I was a newborn infant. The story goes something like this: He had recently graduated from Law School at Duke University and subsequently moved his family to San Jose, California. At that time our family consisted of him, my mother, my sister who was two years older than I was and then me. I was a few weeks old when we made this trip. He said that he drove us across the country to California from Durham, North Carolina, and on that trip all I did was eat, cry, and spit up. He said that my mom was trying to breastfeed me and that I was not tolerating her milk. He went on to say that I was allergic to her milk, even though he had no evidence of this diagnosis other than his interpretation of the events that he had witnessed. He described me as an infant that was constantly crying and vomiting. You would think that someone should have taken that infant to see a doctor, but that did not happen for me. Eventually, my mom put me on some sort of formula that apparently lessened my symptoms and was touted as a cure, by my dad. Looking back now, I can guess that I most likely had reflux, which is common in infancy and does get better as an infant grows older. Still, this is the one memory that always stood out for my dad, and he would recite it over and over. He would always tell this story proudly, as if it were his idea to put me on formula and that this decision was the thing that saved me. I feel like he saw this one parental act as a victory, and since he was absent for so much of my life, he cited this one event as proof of his parental involvement and ability. As an adult now, I know it is rarely a good idea to replace breastmilk with formula, to say nothing about the damage that must have done to my mother's self-esteem, as she was made to feel like she had failed at her fundamental role of feeding her infant. To my knowledge, from that time forward, each of my mother's subsequent babies were raised on formula instead of breast milk.

It seemed that from my early beginning, food took on a central role in my life. My ability to control my food provided me with a strategy to control my childhood and all the turmoil that surrounded our family. My father was always focused on outward appearance – he was all about the package, not necessarily the contents. By the time I was in seventh or eighth grade, my dad had remarried and had subsequently adopted three of his wife's four children. I actually had a stepsister named Kim Fisher! My dad spoke very highly of his new daughter, Kimmie Dawn. Apparently, she was very smart and did well in school. She was one year older than I was, and I remember feeling like I could not compete with her for my dad's attention. On one particular evening with my dad, he pinched some skin on the side of my waist and jiggled it, while laughing. I have no idea how anyone could pinch anything on me, but I do remember that event and the overwhelming feeling that I had to be thinner. I weighed approximately 75 pounds when I started the 7th grade. Still, I was obsessed with weighing myself daily. Daily weight checks became a way for me to feel like I was in control of my life. The narrative that I created in my "Maggie mind" was that I needed to stay thin and attractive so that boys would find me pretty. At that time, I was sure that college was not going to be an option for someone like me, so I determined that my only way out of my mother's house would be to get married.

I am the only one to blame for my addiction and in so many ways I never saw it as a negative thing, until it started to control me. Staying under 105 pounds when you are 5'3" should be an easy task – at least that was what I told myself. I made it all the way through high school and through my first marriage weighing 105 pounds. After my first divorce, I consumed the same meal plan every day. I would have one Tab soft drink and a package of four peanut butter crackers; this seemed like a logical food plan to someone with an eating disorder. Being obsessed with my size also seemed like a logical way to think. When I divorced my first husband, I quickly latched onto my eating disorder for comfort, safety, and support. Within two months, I went from a 105 pounds to 81 pounds. By that time, I had moved back into my mother's house. No one voiced concern over what I was doing to my body, which mirrored our unspoken family code – don't ask and don't tell. We were a family of secrets. Secrets were the common threads that each of us wove together to make up the fabric of our family.

Shortly after reaching 81 pounds, I began to notice that my periods changed. They became irregular with very little flow. At that time, I was working in a department store in the billing department. This was the first job that I ever had as an adult. My life during that time is mostly a blur because I was just existing, not living. For the next few years, I rarely dated and I remained safe and secure with my eating disorder.

Eventually I met Jay. My eating disorder was front and center during my life with Jay. Jay liked me best when I was thin. I am not sure that there was a "too thin" point for him. During my marriage to Jay, getting back to my pre-pregnant weight was something that I immediately focused on after each and every childbirth. I did not gain that much weight with most of my children and the weight that I did gain seemed to melt off me, with little to no effort. When I was pregnant with my second son, Karson, I gained 70 pounds. This was my only completely normal pregnancy, and I don't remember feeling anxious about the weight that I had gained. I was just ecstatic about the fact that I had had a normal pregnancy. Even with this excessive weight gain I went back down to 110 pounds within three months of his birth. By that point, I began to see my eating disorder as normal. I did not understand how or why so many women remained heavy after having a baby. If you starve when you are pregnant and then starve more afterwards, while also taking diet pills, then weight loss should be a breeze! This was the mindset of someone who was controlled by her eating disorder. I was still years away from facing the reality of my addiction.

Anorexia gave me a sense of control over my life. While, so much of my childhood and adolescence were cloaked in chaos, my eating disorder gave me a sense of order. It was the one thing in my life that I could count on, and I held on to it as if it were a lifeline; there were many times when it was all that I had. I will admit that during this time, I was often judgmental of others because my own life was so out of control. The only thing I had control over was my body and my weight, and one of the ways I did that was by using diet pills. It is never a good idea to take diet pills, especially the ones that I took after my first son, Karter, was born. The diet pills that I took were called Dexatrim, and at that time they were sold over the counter in any local drug store. Dexatrim contained Ephedra, an amphetamine-like compound. I never told my husband, Jay, that I was taking them because I felt that he would disapprove. In retrospect, maybe Jay would not have cared that I was taking diet pills because they did help remove my pregnancy weight within the first month of Karter's life.

My eating disorder stayed consistent throughout my marriage to Jay, up until the day when I found out about Jay's secret life. Finding out about Jay's addiction shook me to my core. I felt the pain of betrayal so deep within me that even my eating disorder was not enough to provide me with a sense of control, stability, or relief. This was the first time that my eating disorder and my desire to control my eating did nothing to ease the pain that I was experiencing. Initially, I had no idea what to do, where to go or how to alleviate the pain that I was feeling. God was preparing me for another way of knowing and another way of being…all I could do was just hold on for the ride, because I felt like I was out of options. My faith was all that I had left at that point in my life and somehow, I stepped off the ledge. At first, I knew I was being carried but then, eventually, I did learn to fly.

Over a period of three years, I made the decision to start and then stop my divorce from Jay on three separate occasions. Since November 30th, 1995, the day that Jay's secret was revealed, our entire family had been in therapy. My children and I went to individual therapy, while Jay and I did a lot of couples' therapy. Jay was also doing individual therapy for his addiction. One day, during an intensive therapy weekend Jay and I were doing with our therapist in Florida, Jay began to experience intense feelings of remorse over the realization of how his addiction had impacted our family. As we were walking to the car, he abruptly stopped and put his hand on the car to steady himself. I could see that his eyes were filling with tears and his face was flushed. "Kim, someday after all this is over and I am healed, I am going to take you on a wonderful vacation, because you deserve so much for standing by my side through all of this!" he said. At that time, I was keeping a "Blessings Journal" so that I could record good things that happened to me, in the hopes that I could bring some light into the darkness that had consumed so much of my life during that time. It was a suggestion from my therapist, and I wrote this event in my journal that night. The truth was that I did not want to get a divorce. Even during my darkest moments, I could not imagine my life separate from Jay. I did not want our children to grow up without their father, splitting their time between both of their parents. I prayed every night that Jay would be healed.

My two oldest children, Karter and Mona, both knew much more about the struggles of their parents than children should know. They were both 17 years old and in their senior year in high school when we made the decision to divorce. Karter played baseball for his local high school and during this time one of his teammate's fathers was featured on the local news for having solicited the services of a prostitute. I remember the night this story ran on the local evening news. Karter and I were both watching it together as his friend's father was caught on camera, being arrested at a hotel in the company of a prostitute. In that moment, I know that we were both thinking the same thing – this could have been Jay. The shame that surrounds this type of addiction is pervasive. Sex addiction is considered a controversial term within the medical community, and it is not officially recognized as a diagnosis in the Diagnostic and Statistical Manual of Mental Disorders (DSM is a standardized system for classifying and diagnosing mental disorders, including addiction, which is published by American Psychiatric Association [APA]). Rather, sex addiction is often considered to be a compulsive behavior that causes distress and negative consequences for the individual and for family members. Therefore, finding help and support for Jay and for us as a family was very difficult. In 1995, our children ranged in ages from one year to 14 years of age. Jay had joined a local 12-step group and he was slowly working his way through the 12-steps. During that time Jay wanted to make amends for his behavior, and he talked to the older children about some of the things that he had done related to his addiction that directly impacted them. Each of our kids handled the news differently. Karter and Mona were both angry and wanted to make sure that I did not fall for Jay's missteps, again. Karson seemed to keep his feelings to himself, even though he sometimes commented that he was worried about his dad. He wanted to make sure that his dad knew that he was still loved by all of us. One evening, while Jay was at our house visiting with the kids, Karson snuck out to his dad's car and placed a coffee cup in the driver's seat that he had purchased with his own money. Printed on the cup were the following words: "World's Greatest Dad."

Around Christmas time in 1998, Karter and Mona, both told me that they wanted to talk to me. Mona went first. She told me that Jay had brought a date to a Christmas party that was held at her biological mother's house. Mona's biological mother had worked for Jay as his office manager since moving to North Carolina in 1994. I tried to not react to hearing this news, but inside I knew that my marriage was ending. Karter went next. He told me that one of his teammates from baseball told him that he had seen Jay in the pharmacy shopping with another woman. That was that. The next day I phoned my attorney and told her to remove the previous hold that I had placed on the divorce and to let it proceed through the court system. I never attempted to stop the divorce again.

When I first found out about Jay's secret, we had been married for 17 years. For the next few years, we focused on his recovery. Slowly, we begin to have hope that we were going to come out on the other end of this experience together, as a family. We began to make plans to celebrate our 20th wedding anniversary with a renewal of our wedding vows. I began to make plans for our big event by booking a venue for the celebration and discussing with the wedding planner what we wanted for our big day. Kylie was three years old, and I bought a beautiful headband that she would wear as our flower girl that would sit on her head like a crown. It had white and pink ribbons that cascaded down from the top, and the top of the headband was decorated with white and pink rose buds made out of linen. I often dreamed about how our day would be. This gave me so much hope for our future together as a family. I had Kylie's headband in my bedroom sitting on top of my dresser so that Kylie would not see it and want to use it for playing dress up. I could imagine how Kylie would look all dressed up in her beautiful tea-length dress with her crown of roses on her head. I could physically feel a sense of accomplishment that Jay and I had weathered a catastrophe that would have broken so many other couples and yet, somehow, we had gotten to the other side of this darkness. In my dreams, Jay and I were standing hand in hand surrounded by our beautiful children. This image consumed every inch of my "Maggie mind" for several months as I continued to move forward with the planning of our vow renewal ceremony! This dream kept me focused on our mission to heal Jay, because in the end, we would be together. This dream gave me hope. Eventually, I started to realize that my dream of us as a family was gradually fading from the reality of our everyday lives. It was hard to give up on this dream but eventually it became evident that I needed to cancel the venue reservation. I cancelled the reservation at the same time that I released the hold on my divorce and allowed the court system to take over the processing of our divorce. I gave the precious headband to Kylie and she played dress-up with her crown of roses for several years, never really knowing why it was purchased in the first place. She did eventually wear it for my brother Knox's wedding, where she walked down the aisle as his flower girl.

It was during times like these that my eating disorder helped me focus my energy on something that I could control. I honestly believe that without my addiction, there were some dark times of depression that could have easily ended my life. For the next few months, while the divorce proceeded, I made plans to leave North Carolina. I knew that in order to protect my own sanity, I would have to move myself and our children away from their father.

Around this time, Jay had another relapse of his addiction, and his therapist and I organized an intervention with his family and friends to help force Jay into another treatment facility. Our couples' therapist helped me secure a spot at a treatment facility in California. I pre-paid for the treatment and purchased a plane ticket for Jay, which would force him to leave that very evening. Jay had had several episodes of relapse during his recovery process, which is not unexpected for newly recovering addicts. The difference between this relapse and previous episodes of relapse is that on this occasion I did not manage to secure anyone to cover Jay's medical practice at the hospital. Previous treatment opportunities were planned in advance to allow for me or Jay to get either Jay's partner or another physician to cover his patients at the hospital. This time his partner refused to cover Jay's practice. His exact words to me when I called to ask him if he would cover Jay's practice were, "I have no desire to help that asshole!" I had never heard anyone speak of Jay in this way and I had no way of knowing why his partner was unwilling to help him this time. Regardless, I was not able to secure coverage for Jay's hospital practice and I knew that this would have professional consequences for his career. I immediately had a discussion with our therapist because I was concerned about whether or not we should proceed with the planned intervention, given this new development. Our therapist reminded me that there were repercussions for Jay's behavior and maybe it was time for him to experience consequences in his professional career. The intervention proceeded as planned. It involved our older children, my brother Knox, our couples' therapist, and my friend, Robin, who was, also, a colleague of Jay's. The intervention was a success. Jay agreed to go to treatment and he left that evening from the Charlotte, North Carolina, airport.

By the time Jay left for treatment, we had finalized the mediation process in the courts and Jay had agreed to give me full custody of the children while he would retain periodic visitations. I know that Jay gave up his children because he loved them enough to recognize that it was what was best for them at that moment. Jay was gone to treatment for almost a whole month. During that time, the hospital where Jay practiced became aware that Jay was not available to cover his hospital duties. The hospital proceeded to file charges against Jay for patient abandonment and eventually Jay was required to go before the North Carolina American Medical Association. They determined that he would be held under the jurisdiction of the Impaired Physician Board for a period of 10 years. If Jay remained in good standing during this time, his license would remain active for him to practice medicine, but if he made the decision to move outside the state of North Carolina, the review process would start all over again. For this reason, I made the decision to move myself and our children out of North Carolina to Tennessee. I no longer worried that Jay would follow me.

My youngest brother, Knox, lived in Memphis, Tennessee. He helped me plan our move to Memphis. Knox helped me contact a realtor in Memphis, who helped me find a home for my children and me. I told her that I wanted a house with a pool. In my "Maggie mind," I thought that if we had a house with a pool, the kids would have too much fun to even notice the loss of their dad in their lives. It's evident that my perception of how moving our children away from their father would impact them was distorted by my own emotional struggles.

In the spring of 1999, prior to moving to Memphis, I made the decision to go to treatment for two weeks for my eating disorder. I went to "Shades of Hope," located in Arizona, which was well known for their successes in the treatment of eating disorders. I knew that I could no longer rely on my addiction to keep the pain of my life from consuming me. I knew that I had to heal myself and show up for my kids before we headed to Tennessee.

I had many powerful experiences during my time in treatment. I arrived at treatment thinking that I was practically already recovered from my eating disorder, since I had been in therapy for the previous three years. However, I quickly realized that I was still being deceived by my addiction. One day during treatment, we did a deep breathing exercise accompanied by an intense drumming session. We were each positioned on a mat in a dimly lit room with loud drumming sounds, as we were guided through a meditation for a two-hour period. During this time, I could feel that I was struggling to complete the exercise because I was still trying to control the outcome. Finally, after what seemed like a long time, I allowed myself to melt into the experience. Only then did I understand what I was holding on to. Although, by the time I went to treatment, I had already made the decision to end my marriage to Jay, I was still struggling to say goodbye to him. I realized that this was because, deep down inside, I had been waiting to finally say "hello." Since he began his recovery from addiction, I had secretly felt a sense of excitement, believing that I would finally uncover Jay's true authentic self for the very first time. But in that meditation, I realized that I needed to let go of the hope that Jay would ever change or that we as a couple would survive his addiction. As much as I wanted and needed Jay, I needed me more. During this breathing exercise, I started the painful process of letting go of Jay and of us together as a couple. I had to untether myself from Jay. I began to realize that controlling my recovery was the same thing as having an addiction. I learned that my need to stay in control was keeping me trapped in an addictive pattern. The truth is, I was secretly hoping to go through the steps of recovery while still maintaining control of my diet. At that point, I honestly believed that I metabolized food differently than everyone else and therefore had to control what I ate or I would get fat. Addiction distorts your thinking, and letting go of this thinking pattern was the ultimate exercise in trust. I had to trust that I could let go of it and of my attempts at control, and not fall apart. My time at treatment helped me begin a plan of recovery that would guide and support me for the rest of my life.

The shadow side of my addiction was often difficult to recognize. It was a trusted friend and companion that had accompanied me throughout my life. I thought of it as a blessing, because it allowed me to remain thin, despite multiple pregnancies. It took me many years to realize the immense impact that my eating disorder had on both my body and on my multiple miscarriages. If I was starving my body, wasn't I also starving my babies? Despite seeing multiple high-risk pregnancy specialists, I never had anyone mention to me that my thin frame may be unsuitable for a healthy pregnancy. I never had any healthcare provider ask me about my nutrition status or in any way hint that this might be an issue worth closer scrutiny. It may be that my eating disorder had no impact on the miscarriages that I had throughout my early adulthood, but I cannot imagine that it was not a participating factor. For most of my adulthood I was angry that my body did not work like other women's bodies and allow me to carry a pregnancy to term. The realization that perhaps it was not my body, but my addiction, that put my pregnancies and my life at risk, was a daunting revelation, but one that I can now clearly recognize as real.

Over the first three years after the events that unfolded after Jay's secrets were revealed, I not only had a lot of therapy, but I also attended multiple 12-step groups. It was very difficult to find 12-step groups specifically focused on eating disorders, so I went to open Alcoholic Anonymous, Overeaters Anonymous and AL-Anon groups (an international mutual aid organization for people who have been impacted by another person's addiction). These 12-steps meetings were a lifeline for me during the first few years of my own recovery. They taught me that Jay's addiction was not something that I could control or heal. They allowed me a safe space to heal myself, instead. I am forever grateful for all of the tools that I learned in these meetings and in therapy, which allowed me to create a different life for me and for my children.

Our move to Memphis felt like a new beginning. Within the first year that we moved it became obvious that my middle son, Karson, was falling into a pattern of addiction. Karson told me at the age of 12, while we were still living in North Carolina, that he had been using marijuana with some of his friends. I was shocked. At that time all I could focus on was getting us to Memphis. Karson's journey with addiction ended up consuming most of his teenage years. After multiple attempts to get him the help that he needed, only to have him relapse after coming home, I made the agonizing decision to place him into a year-long inpatient facility in Memphis called Memphis Recovery Center (MRC). MRC became the answer that Karson needed to get clean and stay clean. He left MRC at the age of 17 years of age, entered his senior year of high school and never relapsed again.

Ten years later on January 24, 2011, at 8:31 AM, I received the following email from my son, Karson:

Hey mom,

I don't know if you remember this day as vividly as I do, but it was 10 years ago today that you gave me the greatest gift that anyone has ever and will ever give me. As we were driving to MRC that morning, I remember stopping at a stoplight and looking out the window and thinking to myself, "I could open this door right now and run away and just never come back" but I literally did not even have the motivation to run. At that point in my life, I felt completely defeated and simply was out of ideas on how to be happy. I was a shell of a person, and I never want to forget how hopeless and empty I felt that day. I had no idea what was going to happen from then on, and I don't think you did either, but this day, 10 years ago, was the day that I got to start my life over. I don't know why you never gave up on me, mom, nor will I ever know how difficult it was for you to watch me destroy myself, but I truly believe that if I did not get clean when I did, I would not be where I am today and likely would still be living in an institution somewhere or not living at all. Thank you, mom, more than I could ever say. I have come a long way since that 16-year-old shell that walked into MRC and I am proud of the man that I am today and I hope that you can say the same thing. Tonight, I'll be picking up my 10-year medallion at my meeting and I just want you to know that at 9pm when we close the meeting in a circle, I will be sending all the love and thanks that I can to you, because nothing I have accomplished or done since that day could have been done without you. I am so blessed to have you as my mother and will never forget all that you have done for me. Thank you, mom, and I love you.

Love,
Karson

Karson has shared with me over the years about how his addiction impacted him. He recognizes that he had many insecurities in his life that helped to fuel his addiction from an early age. Karson went on to finish his PhD in Bioenergetics and is now an Associate Professor in Cancer Biology and Molecular Medicine with a major academic medical center in North Carolina. He remains an active member in Narcotics Anonymous.

Narcotics Anonymous and other 12-step programs are built on the foundations outlined by the founding program Alcoholics Anonymous (AA). The 12-steps of AA are focused on personal accountability and the constant maintenance of a fearless moral inventory of oneself to ensure sobriety. As an addict, I wholeheartedly support the steps and traditions in 12-step programs, but I remain steadfast in my belief that addictive behaviors and tendencies are often perpetuated within families for generations because of unspoken secrets. Author Scott Peck wrote the book *People of the Lie*, which highlights the ways that secrets permeate families, leaving pain and destruction along the way, because no one is willing or able to speak the truth. For years, I have reminded my children that secrets will kill. When secrets go unspoken, generation after generation, the family will be forever burdened by that secret until someone is brave enough to step up and speak the truth. Once truth is spoken, the secret loses its power. I grew up in a family where there were so many secrets, that I became accustomed to the response of "I don't know" every time I had the courage to ask a question of an adult family member. I had so many questions about events in my life and in the life of both of my parents, and even today many of those questions remain unanswered. Questions like, why was my mother raised by the town doctor's family, while her two sisters were raised with their parents? What happened to my dad's father and why did I not ever meet him? Why was my dad's brother raised by another family, while my dad stayed with his mom? I learned from an early age to not question anything that was happening around me. One of the many gifts that I have received over the years is to question everything and to NEVER be afraid of the truth, because the spoken word is powerful! These gifts are the same tools that I have used throughout my adult life that have allowed me the opportunity to heal many of my own childhood wounds. For the three years after finding out about Jay's addiction and before I made the decision to file for a divorce, Jay and I tried to piece together his own family secrets, so that he too could heal his childhood wounds and, perhaps, be healed from his addiction. For three years, healing Jay became our mission, as a couple.

After the sting of Jay's betrayal had time to lessen, while we were still together, I began to focus all my energy into finding a way to heal Jay. We would often lay in bed at night, after all of the kids were asleep, and try to put the pieces of Jay's childhood together to try and uncover the many secrets that haunted even his "picture perfect family." I had so many questions, and I very quickly realized that Jay remembered very little about the key players in his family. Jay's family consisted of his parents and one older sister. Both sets of his grandparents were active during their childhood and during the early years of our marriage. Jay had almost no memories from his early childhood. Initially he told me that he had no memories at all before the age of around four to five. Jay's paternal grandfather passed away when our two oldest children were still very young. After his grandfather's passing, we would spend a lot of time at his grandparents' house with his family. We became aware, while trying to help his grandmother get her house cleaned out, that his grandfather had stashed decades of pornographic magazines in their attic. His grandfather had arranged the magazines in the attic in such a way that would allow him the ability to view them as needed. When this secret became known to the family, I remember Jay's dad talking to his two sisters, suggesting that perhaps their mother, Jay's grandmother, had put the magazines there for her husband. Both of Jay's aunts dismissed this theory as totally false, without any hesitation. However, Jay's dad was unwilling to believe that his dad would have put such magazines in the attic himself. We were never able to figure out how the magazines got into the attic, and the grandsons were quickly tasked with removing the stacks of magazines, which were later burned in the trash pile.

Jay's paternal grandfather was a very religious man, who attended his local church every Sunday. The thought that perhaps he used pornography for any reason was immediately never discussed again after this incident. Jay and I continued to try and delve into his own stored memories from his childhood. After several unsuccessful attempts to try and remember his childhood, Jay suddenly began remembering some events from his childhood that involved both him and his sister. When he first revealed these events out loud to me, we both fell silent. In the following days, Jay would begin to cry as the memories of these events started to bubble to the surface and he began to share them, out loud, with me. Over the next few nights, we diligently tried to piece together his childhood based on his newly emerged memories. Jay continued to remember more and more, and we both felt hopeful for the first time since his addiction had been revealed to me that we might get to the source of it and be able to finally help heal him. Then one night, everything changed when I suggested to Jay that since we now knew some truths about his childhood, we needed to talk to his parents and confirm with them what we now knew. As soon as I said the words, "We need to talk to your parents now," Jay held his breath. It was like he had stopped breathing, then he quickly replied, "NO, absolutely not!"

Jay's decision to not tell his parents was the beginning of the end of our marriage. I knew it in that moment, but it took me a little time to process the reality of my marriage ending. This event occurred a few short months before my talk with Karter and Mona revealed to me that Jay had already moved on with his life without me. Speaking the truth in a family of secrets is hard. Jay was determined to heal from his addiction and still allow the secrets in his family to remain, forever, unspoken. He did not understand that healing is only possible through speaking the truth – the whole truth. I told him that I was unwilling to carry this secret for him, and he would have to find a way to reconcile this fact for himself. I struggled with whether or not to reveal Jay's secret in this book. Ultimately, I decided that the secret does not belong to me, therefore I made the decision to not reveal it. That secret belongs to Jay and only he can heal his own truth. My decision to not include Jay's secret is founded on one fundamental truth – secrets have no power when they are spoken out loud, but you have to have the courage to speak them.

Finding out about Jay's addiction made me question each and every event in our marriage. Every experience in our marriage had to be reexamined through the lens of his addiction. I began to understand that his addiction was about so much more than his need to seek sexual encounters outside of our marriage. His addiction meant that he was not present, truly present, for me and for our children. One Christmas, while we were living in the mountains of West Virginia, we had planned a trip back to the Huntington area over the Christmas holiday to visit our families. At that time, both our clinic practice and Jay's hospital practice did not allow for much flexibility in our work schedules. We planned to head home to see our families after we both finished work on the day before Christmas Eve. Jay called me that afternoon and told me that he was going to have to work later than he had expected and he wanted me to go ahead and take the kids to his parents' house and he would follow later that night. I remember telling him that I was willing to wait for him so that we could all go together, but he insisted that I not wait for him. I told him that I was concerned about the weather forecast, which warned of freezing temperatures and heavy snow overnight. Reluctantly, I left after work with our children. The drive to his parents' house was very difficult due to the severe snowstorm that hit the area that evening. After I had safely arrived at Jay's parents' house, I quickly got the children to bed and then headed to bed myself. I remember lying in bed, feeling extremely frustrated with Jay's decision to put work above his family, yet again. Jay arrived sometime in the middle of the night. I voiced my frustration the next day to Jay, but his defense was that he had a critically ill patient that he had to take care of before he felt comfortable leaving the hospital. After the revelation of his secret, he later confessed that he had not had an emergency at work that night but had instead stopped in

Charleston to visit a prostitute before heading to his parents' house for the holidays.

There was another event that occurred just a few short months after our last child was born. We had decided to take the children to the beach. We ended up going to one of the beaches on the coast of North Carolina. Shortly after arriving, we got the kids ready to take them to the pool. Jay offered to go and get everyone some food from a local fast-food restaurant while I stayed with the kids at the pool. Jay was gone for more than three hours before returning with food for the kids. By this time the kids were famished and ready to eat and I was sick with worry. When Jay finally arrived, his explanation for his delay was that he had gotten lost on his way back to our hotel. After knowing his secret, I re-evaluated this event. I knew that this was yet another time that Jay put his addiction before his family.

There were also two instances when Kylie was an infant, when she had to be rushed to the emergency department because she was having difficulty breathing. Kylie had been born with a malformation in her lower jaw that caused a severe narrowing in her esophagus. We did not know about the defect until she was six years old and had her first set of dental x-rays completed. As an infant, any upper respiratory illness Kylie had could very quickly become an emergency. One evening she was having trouble breathing and I paged Jay at the hospital and asked him to come home. He assured me that Kylie was fine and that he would be home as soon as he could. I called him back a few minutes later and told him that I was taking her to the ER (emergency room). Jay encouraged me not to take her and again told me that I was over-reacting. Our oldest son, Karter, had recently gotten his learner's permit, but he had never driven at night. I told Karter that he was going to have to drive us to the hospital because I was concerned that I might need to perform rescue breaths on Kylie if her breathing became any more labored. I remember how scared Karter was as I encouraged him to go faster and faster. When Karter finally turned into the driveway to the ER, he did not even slow down and as we hit the first speed bump, we all bounced out of our seats, but Karter got us safely to the hospital. When we arrived, the hospital staff immediately placed an oxygen mask on Kylie, to stabilize her oxygen levels. The kids and I were all so scared. Finally, Jay arrived. I was so angry with him. It felt like we always came last in his life. Jay was constantly concerned about what his peers would think of him if one of his children needed to be taken to the hospital. This was yet another time when his other priorities came before his children. Kylie was diagnosed with a viral illness and put on medication to help support her breathing through the illness.

    Jay's addiction took priority in his life. This often caused him to become distracted when our children were under his direct supervision. There were at least two events when Jay actually lost our middle son, Karson. Karson was an extremely curious child and required constant supervision. Jay had taken both Karter and Karson to a professional baseball game and after the game was over and the crowd was exiting the stadium, Karson got separated from his dad and brother. A good Samaritan found Karson and Jay was immediately summoned to the press box to retrieve his son. This event scared Jay. Jay had tears in his eyes as he was telling me about this experience after he came home. This event occurred prior to my knowing about Jay's addiction. At that time Jay decided on his own that he would not take Karson with him to professional games for the next one to two years until Karson was able to sit still and stay in his seat. Initially, Jay blamed Karson for the events that led to him being separated from his dad. After Jay's secret was revealed, Jay confessed to me that he had promised to take the boys to meet the players after the game and that Karson had bounced out of his seat to go meet the players and was quickly out of sight, while Jay became distracted by an attractive woman who was, according to Jay, "dressed provocatively."

Another time, when we had taken our kids to Disney World when Kylie was only a few weeks old. Most of my attention during this time was devoted to Kylie. At one point I sat down on a bench to breastfeed Kylie, while Jay took the other kids to go on one of the rides that was close to where I was seated. After about 20 minutes, Jay arrived, flushed with frustration, and holding tightly to Karson's hand. Karson had once again slipped away from his father's gaze, leaving Jay frantically trying to find him. Eventually, Karson was spotted and returned to his dad. Later, Jay would reveal to me that he had once again become distracted by an attractive woman.

These events highlight the power that addiction can and does have over an individual. Jay is a kind and loving father who would never cause harm to his children. His addiction had affected him by not only putting himself in harm's way but, he also put his children in harm's way. After knowing about Jay's secret, each and every event that I had previously questioned in our relationship was again reviewed through the lens of his addiction. Addiction is never just about the addict or even always about the addiction. Anyone that exists in the same world as an addict will always be viewed as less important than the addiction, by the addict. This was my new reality.

What I learned about Jay's addiction and how it impacted us as a family was complicated by my own addiction. Maybe Jay gave us the best pieces of himself that he had available to give us. Maybe my own addiction compounded the impact of Jay's addiction on us as a couple and us as a family. I cannot judge Jay for those things that he had no control over any more than I can judge myself for how my own shortcomings impacted our family. What I do know is that I got the best that Jay could give to me because without him I would not have the four children that I bore and the one child that we all chose.

By the time I moved to Memphis, I had been in therapy with the same therapist for several years. Therapy was a lifeline for me in so many ways and together with my therapist we embarked on a journey to heal my childhood wounds and allow me the opportunity to live my life, authentically. It involved not only time with my therapist, but journaling, introspection, and attendance at appropriate 12-step groups, when needed. After several years in therapy had passed, the time came for me to prepare for my reconstruction process. The reconstruction process involves bringing all the pieces of one's life together that have constructed the individual so that they can clearly see the pieces that have formed them as an adult. This process allows the individual to move from their wounded self to an identity of freedom and authenticity. I was ecstatic to be moving toward my own reconstruction!

I spent a few months gathering pictures, dates, journaling and compiling a large collage of my life, from birth to present day. After everything was compiled for the reconstruction process, I spent some time with my therapist discussing the important milestones that I had identified, explored, and worked through. The reconstruction process was then shared with a support group, made up of family and friends, as my therapist directed the reconstruction process, which was a journey through the life events that had shaped me. This process was restorative and transformative as we spent two days journeying through my life events surrounded by my support team, my family and therapist. For me, this felt much like my dissertation defense for my doctorate degree in that each occurred after a long and grueling process of intense work! While the work for my dissertation defense was academically driven and my reconstruction was emotionally driven, they both occurred simultaneously. As important as my PhD degree was to me, I am not sure it would have occurred without the work that I did to heal the brokenness inside myself. I am forever grateful for this experience and for those who participated and supported me throughout both of these accomplishments!

I am grateful for the secrets in my life that have been revealed. When both my parents and Jay's parents were children, keeping secrets was often viewed as the best path forward for our families. I can still remember how my mom instructed us, as children, to not tell anyone about our dad's drunken episodes. Secrets were meant to stay secrets. For me now, speaking the secret out loud makes it disappear into the world as a whisper. Gone is the power that it once held over me and over us, as a family. I often wonder how different both mine and Jay's lives would have been without the secrets that came from our respective families. My hope is that my children will not carry forward any secrets from either of their parents' pasts. This is the legacy that I want to leave for my children.

For me, therapy has been a gift. Without the opportunity to heal my own childhood wounds, I would not be able to become the authentic, whole person that I am today. Through therapy, I have come to realize that while mine and Jay's addictions hurt us, as individuals and us as a family, they also became the call to action that we both needed to take the steps to heal our childhood wounds so we could change and both become the better version of ourselves that we are today. Healing from an addiction is an arduous task and it is rarely a smooth and easy process. For me, my addiction has provided me with the opportunity to choose the way that I want to exist and live in this world. Change is possible.

LESSON EIGHT

Our children will teach us, if we let them

Children and their parents have a symbiotic relationship with one another. Children need parents to love, guide and protect them, and parents need children to teach them how to parent. When you have absent parents or parents who are unable to see the many lessons being taught to them by their children, then the beneficial relationship that was formed before the child was even born, is broken. The magical reality about children is that they are willing to teach us the same lesson over and over again, giving each of us the time that we need to learn from them.

Growing up with four siblings taught me a lot about myself. Our birth order went as follows: Karla was the oldest, I was two years younger than Karla, Keith was one and a half years younger than me, Kris was three years younger than Keith, and finally Knox was four years younger than Kris. The age span from the oldest to the youngest was 10 years. Karla assumed the maternal role in our family, out of necessity. The lack of available parental guidance and support was obvious to all of us from a very early age. My experience as a child was one of complete and utter fear. I earned the nickname "cry-baby" because I seemed to cry in nearly every photo taken of me during my childhood.

I learned very early to feel insecure about my family, my parents, and our ability to be safe and secure. I frequently felt like an outsider within my own family, as my siblings appeared to lack the same fears and concerns about our family that I experienced.

As children we never discussed with each other any worries that we had about either of our parents. We never discussed what it was like for us when our dad would schedule a time to pick us up and often never arrive. As Karla and I grew older, we began visiting our dad less frequently during our childhood. Mostly, because we could never depend on him to actually show up. Eventually, the only ones who would wait for Dad to come and pick them up for a weekend visit were Keith and Kris. For the first five years of my youngest brother Knox's life, my dad denied being the biological father. Therefore, Knox never went to visit our dad during this time. There were many times when Keith and Kris would be sitting on the curb, in front of our house, waiting for our dad to come and pick them up. It would start to get dark, and they would eventually pick up their little suitcase and come back in the house. I don't recall ever talking about these things as a family. My mom had taught us from a young age that family business should stay within the family. The mantra for our family was 'Don't ask, don't tell.' So, I learned that I should not discuss anything with anyone, not even my siblings. Apparently, this was a lesson that we all understood.

In retrospect, although I felt like I was the only one of my siblings who felt afraid, we were all traumatized by the instability of our childhood. As children, we all counted on our older sister, Karla, to provide us with the stability that we were lacking in our everyday lives. But Karla was just a child herself and was not equipped to meet the many needs of her four younger siblings. Now, as adults, we all realize the profound impact that she had on our lives when we were children. Karla assumed the parental role in our lives, even while she herself was still only in grade school. Karla was, almost exclusively, the primary caretaker for our youngest brother, Knox. Before she headed to school each morning, she made sure that Knox had been fed and that he had on a clean diaper. She would put him in his bouncy seat as we stepped out the door, leaving him alone with our mother while we attended school. Even as a third grader, I can recall coming home from school and finding Knox in the same spot where we had left him that morning. My mother often struggled with severe depression, and as an eight-year-old, I was concerned that she wouldn't take care of Knox while we were at school. I don't know if this impression was founded on fact or fear, but I worried that our mom was not capable of caring for Knox while we were gone. As soon as Karla arrived home each day, she immediately assumed the role of taking care of Knox. Karla had a best friend named Tina who lived across the street, and she frequently took Knox along when she visited. As Knox transitioned into toddlerhood, Tina and her family embraced him as one of their own. They even designated a bottom drawer in their kitchen specifically for Knox, filling it with snacks so he could easily grab his treats while at their home. As a young child, Knox regarded Karla as if she were his mother, and in many ways, she truly was.

Karla married Gavin, the love of her life, on August 25, 2001, after leaving a 17-year abusive marriage to her first husband. Karla and Gavin had dated, previously, when they were in high school. I first met Gavin when I was 15 years old. My boyfriend and I went on a double date with Karla and Gavin to the bowling alley. I vividly remember observing them together. I could see the obvious love that they shared with each other; however, they ultimately ended their relationship. At that time, Karla never shared with me the details surrounding their break-up. I had assumed that it was because it was what she desired for herself. Fast forward almost 30 years later, they found each other again and got married. During a recent conversation with my sister, she admitted to me that Gavin had asked her to marry him when they were teenagers, but she had turned him down because she felt like she was not good enough for him. Hearing her say this about herself actually shocked me. I never imagined that Karla lacked self-confidence. Karla had raised us. She put herself through college and earned a master's degrees in elementary education! She was a greatly respected teacher to hundreds of children. How could she not see what everyone else saw?

The most shocking part of Karla's revelation was that she felt exactly like me. I, too, turned down someone's proposal early in my life because I felt that he deserved someone better. Most of my own insecurities stemmed from my comparison to my big sister, Karla. I was constantly being compared to her, both academically and physically. In my eyes, I was never able to measure up to her. I came to understand that Karla's childhood was also missing many valuable pieces, as well. Somehow, she could not see herself the way the rest of her siblings saw her, as the person who was always and would always be there to take care of us. She was the responsible, capable one. This is what happens to children when parents are absent. Karla had parented all of us, but there was no one to parent her.

When my youngest brother, Knox, was in his early 20s, I took custody of him from the State of Florida. Knox had struggled with alcoholism and drug abuse since his early adolescence. He had moved to Florida after graduating from high school. In 1987, he was arrested for his third DUI (driving under the influence). At that time, the State of Florida was willing to release him to an adult who would assume custody of him, rather than put him in jail. My mother had refused to go to Florida to get him, so I went. I don't remember the details as to why my mother would not go to get Knox, but given her struggles with depression, I presumed that she was not mentally capable to help him at that time. I had to appear before a judge and swear to take personal responsibility of Knox and to assist him with getting the help he needed for his drug and alcohol addictions. At that time, I was living in Mississippi, where Jay had taken his first job after finishing his fellowship in Kentucky. We had only recently moved to Mississippi, and Karter and Karson were both still settling into their new environment after my recent pregnancy loss, subsequent surgery and lengthy hospital stay. Our lives at that time were very hectic, but leaving Knox in Florida was not an option for me.

Once Knox moved into our home, I set up rules he had to follow in order for him to continue to be able to stay with us. He had been ordered by the State of Florida to complete community service, so we got him a volunteer opportunity with the local Salvation Army. He, also, started going to an outpatient treatment facility to help him deal with his addictions. I don't have many memories regarding whether he experienced periods of relapse or if his recovery was straightforward after moving in with us.

At that point in my life, I saw Knox as a child that I had to mother. I was fiercely protective of my own children and wanted to shield them from any inappropriate behaviors that might arise from my decision to have Knox live with us.

I became pregnant again soon after Knox moved in with us. My pregnancy with Kaiden was fraught with complications that often consumed me, both mentally and physically. I had weekly ultrasounds in both Mississippi with my gynecologist and in Memphis with the perinatal specialist. Knox's help and support for my young sons during this time, was invaluable to us as a family. As Knox's recovery continued so did his commitment to our family and our commitment to him.

After Knox settled into his new life with our family, our relationship became even closer. One day Knox asked to talk to me privately. During our conversation, he told me that he was gay and that this secret, more than anything else, had caused him great pain throughout his life. He revealed that his sexuality was the impetus for his long history with drug and alcohol abuse. To this day, I so regret my response to his revelation. At that time in my life, I remained firm in my conviction that being gay was a choice and that it was a choice that he should not be making. My understanding of sexual identity was still being dictated by my small-town Baptist church upbringing.

I was unable to listen to him with my whole open heart, despite the fact that when I was a senior in high school, my dear cousin, Karl, had come out to me as gay — back in 1974! Karl and I were the same age. He was the son of my mother's younger sister. We were very close. We lived in neighboring towns and went to the same junior high and high school. One day when I was at his house, I noticed some marks on his back. He admitted to me that his father had hit him with a belt. He told me that his dad was very angry with him for being gay and that this anger often came out in a fury of abuse for even a minor infraction. At that time, I did not fully understand what it meant to be gay, but I immediately recognized that what my uncle had done to Karl was unacceptable. I tried to convince Karl to tell someone at our school, but he refused. Karl, eventually, left our small town soon after he graduated from our high school and he, rarely returned. When I moved to Memphis in 1999, Karl and I reconnected; he had been living and working in Memphis for several years. I had an opportunity to talk to him about his childhood and his decision to share with me about his sexuality, while we were still in high school. He understood that I reacted in the only way that I knew how, and he held no animosity toward me. We had both grown up in similar small towns, with the same small-town mindset. Karl had contracted AIDS several years prior to 1999 and he was by this time working with a pharmaceutical company to help others with the disease get the help that they needed. His work was very important to him. A few years after we had reconnected in Memphis, Karl made the decision to move back home to our small town in West Virginia. Each time I went to West Virginia to visit my family, we would always get together to catch up. On one occasion, I asked him why he decided to move back home. He told me that he wanted to come home to heal the many wounds he had with his dad. He also confessed to me that he had come home to die. Just a few short years later, I received a phone call from my sister, telling me that Karl had passed away in his sleep after a brief respiratory illness. I am unaware of how things ended between him and his dad, but I do know that he healed some deep wounds with his older brother.

I had been given so many opportunities to open up my mind and my understanding of what it meant to be gay, but I had failed to listen with my whole open heart. Fast forward to the year 2000, the universe gave me another opportunity to learn. At that time, I was living in Memphis and my oldest daughter, Mona, was attending college at Appalachian State University in North Carolina. One evening, she called me and asked if I could meet her in Hickory, North Carolina, sometime soon to discuss something important. She requested that I come alone, without her two youngest siblings. That was all the information that I got from her, but I could definitely hear the tension in her voice – I knew this was serious.

I made plans to meet her that coming weekend. I don't remember what I did with Kaiden and Kylie that weekend, but Mona and I met at the hotel in Hickory, that I had booked for the weekend. I arrived first. When she arrived, I could see the look of absolute terror on her face. I tried hard to stay calm. I was sitting on the bed propped up on pillows, and Mona lay across the foot of the bed on her stomach. I was tense, but focused on her. Mona had been through some difficult times lately and she had, only recently, finally settled into school. I had such pain in my heart for her and I just wanted her college experience to be positive.

I was squeezing my own hands to try and keep from bursting into a puddle of tears from the tension that had quickly filled our room. I said to Mona, "Honey, you can say anything that you need to say, I am here for you!" But inside I was so afraid of what she was going to tell me. All she had done since arriving to the hotel was cry. She seemed inconsolable. She finally started to talk. She talked about some events that had happened at school and then she put her head down on the bed and continued to sob. At this point I was honestly thinking that something awful had happened and that I was going to have to help her hide a body or cover up some crime! These were my actual thoughts, as my fear began to escalate.

After what seemed like an hour, she lifted her head and through her sobs she said, "I'm GAY!" I just nodded and quietly said, "Okay." Then she looked at me and said, "That's what I wanted to tell you – I'm gay!" I said, "Oh my GOD, of course you're gay. I thought you had killed someone and that I was going to have to help you hide a body!" She just looked at me and smiled, then we both started to laugh. I told her that I had always known that she was gay, and it would not have mattered to me one way or the other. Then we hugged. Finally, all the lessons that had been brought to me by my cousin, Karl, and my brother, Knox, allowed me to gift my daughter with acceptance and understanding. I am forever grateful to both of them for helping me be there for my beautiful daughter at the exact moment that she needed me.

My own children have taught me so much over the years. At times, I learned the lesson very quickly. Karter was born in 1981 and Karson followed in 1984. Karson was a very precocious child. After having such a calm and obedient child, like Karter, Karson was very quickly a full-time job just to keep him safe. Karson started pre-school when he was three years old. One day he came home and told me that he could not go back to school unless I brought him to school in a car seat. It seems that the teacher had read a book to the children about car seat safety, and he was convinced that he could not go back to school and would not go back to school unless we got him a car seat. At that time, car seats were available, but they were not mandatory, like they are today. Even as a child, when Karson was committed to something, he was relentless. His dad and I both knew that there was only one path forward when it came to Karson. After trying to reason with him, his dad and I both conceded, and Jay went to the store to get him a car seat. Karson happily returned to school the next day and he proudly announced to his teacher that he had come to school in his new car seat. Looking back now it is hard to imagine that I did not already have my children in car seats but that was a valuable lesson that I learned from my three-year-old son. I remain eternally grateful for this lesson.

One of the most important life lessons that I ever learned came from a little girl who I met at work and I never even know her name. Throughout the week, I traveled from North Carolina to Charlottesville, Virginia, to work on my doctorate degree, while on weekends, I served as a Lactation Consultant at Carolinas Medical Center in Charlotte, North Carolina, completing two 12-hour shifts each weekend. One Saturday night around 2 a.m., I was making my rounds on the labor and delivery floor. As I walked by one of the corner rooms, I could hear what I thought to be a small child being spanked or hit by someone with an angry voice. Without hesitation, I immediately entered the room to find a mother lying in bed with her new baby in the bassinette beside her. The father of the newborn was in the room along with a little girl who appeared to be two to three years of age. I startled everyone when I entered the room so abruptly. I immediately approached the exhausted mom and introduced myself to see if she needed anything. I then turned my attention to the father. I congratulated the father on the birth of his new baby. I also made a few comments about how the birth of a baby could often be a very stressful time for a family and I told him that I would be happy to take their oldest daughter to visit the babies in the nursery and give the family some private time to spend with their new baby. The father appeared surprised by both my appearance into the room and my offer to take his oldest daughter, but he immediately thanked me for the help and allowed me to take his oldest daughter with me. I lifted the little girl into my arms, and we left the room.

The little girl was happy to go with me. We made our way to the nursery to look at all of the babies who, at that time, were not rooming in with their mothers. I could visibly see the red marks on her arm where her father had either grabbed her arm or hit her. I had no idea whether this was typical behavior for this father, but my mind quickly drifted to a place of darkness for this little girl and for her new baby sister. But what could I do? After visiting the babies, we went back to my office where I had some dolls that were used to demonstrate to new mothers how to hold a baby when breastfeeding. We sat in the floor of my office and played with the dolls. She did not talk very much and what words she did speak were difficult for me to understand. I asked her several times what her name was but I was unable to decipher what she was saying to me. I had some snacks in the office that I shared with her and after eating, we walked up and down the halls of the hospital, hand in hand, while I chatted. I took her to visit each of the nurses who were working on the floor that night. A couple of the nurses gave her some candy that they had in their pockets. I kept her with me for about two hours before walking back toward the room where her parents were staying with her new sister. Before I took her back in the room, I picked her up and whispered in her ear, "You are loved." She looked at me, smiled and gave me the biggest hug.

I realized in that moment that I could make a difference in someone's life by just being present with them in the moment. My natural impulse had always been to rescue anyone and everyone who needed my help. This was the first time that I considered how just my being present, in each moment, could impact someone. I think often about that little girl and even though I never knew her name, she taught me so much. I did not have to rescue everyone; I just needed to rescue myself. As soon as the social worker came in that same morning, I explained to her what I had witnessed so that she could follow up with the family to ensure that the family had the support that they needed. After my encounter with that little girl, I approached every patient differently. I learned to listen more. I tried to be mindful of my presence in the moment without the distraction of thinking ahead to the workload in front of me. I took one of my business cards and on the back, I wrote the following statement: "When the time is right, my child, when the time is right." Before entering each patient's room, I read this card and it helped remind me that while I was at that time dealing with a lot of sadness in my own life, I was not alone, and I could still be of help and of service to others. So many years have passed since that experience. I still have the card that I wrote on and I still think about that little girl and the valuable lesson she taught me.

When a parent has multiple children, they parent each child differently. At least, this was my own experience. I observed that I was a different parent with each of my children because I was different. They would often fuss because I did something for one of the kids that I had not previously done for them. In those moments, I would remind them that I was becoming a different mother with each passing day. The lessons that Kylie would teach me took me a long time to recognize. I clung to Kylie during my divorce from her father and in that moment, I don't think that I could have done anything differently. After all, I was in survival mode. Kylie was only 1 year old when I first learned of Jay's secret. After Kylie was born, I had severe postpartum depression. I had had it after Kaiden's birth as well, but it was not as severe as it was after Kylie was born.

Kylie was a fussy baby and the only thing that seemed to soothe her was to breastfeed. She and I had made a nest on the couch for the first few weeks, maybe months, of her life. I don't remember how or who cared for my other kids during this dark time, as I fell into a deep depression. When Kylie was about eight weeks old, I tried to explain to Jay what I was feeling. Jay's response went something like this: "There is something wrong with you, you need to see a psychiatrist!" Yes, indeed, I did need to see someone, but I never did. There was a time, right before I was supposed to return to school for the upcoming semester, that I had repeated thoughts of harming myself. I had even devised a plan on how I would end the pain that I was experiencing. I considered jumping off the deck of our back patio, which was over two stories high, in an attempt to end both my life and Kylie's. Because Kylie only wanted me, I thought that I was doing the most loving thing I could do by deciding to take her with me when I jumped. I thank God every day that I was too exhausted to even get up and implement my plan. Eventually I was able to think more clearly, and slowly the depression lifted enough for me to see it for what it was. Looking back now, it is scary to think that I was actually planning to kill both myself and my infant daughter. I have no idea whether or not I would have gone through with it, if it weren't for the exhaustion that had taken over my body. It had taken me a long time to get the courage to tell Jay how I was feeling, and his response left me feeling even more hopeless. Postpartum depression is real and it is a very insidious disorder that goes undiagnosed in so many new mothers. Even though I was aware that I had experienced severe depression after Kaiden was born, I neglected to recognize the symptoms when they occurred again after having Kylie. As a healthcare provider I was aware of the symptoms of postpartum depression and of the fact that once a mother experiences these symptoms, subsequent pregnancies can often manifest with more severe symptoms. However, while in the depths of depression, I lost my ability to discern and evaluate my own diagnosis. I had had several doctor visits for both myself and Kylie during those first few weeks and months, and my husband was a physician, and, yet, my depression was allowed to reach a critical point. I never forgot this experience and it later directed much of the care that I provided to the moms that I saw in my professional life. I always made a point to discuss depression with all of the new mothers that I saw professionally in the hope that this awareness could help someone experiencing depression reach out for help and assistance.

In 2007, Kylie was 13 years old when she had her first seizure. It was Sunday morning on June 14, 2007. Kylie had spent the night with her friend, Hailey, and I had gone to pick her up about 8 a.m. so that she could have time to get ready for church. She was in my bathroom, and I had stepped out to get her hairbrush for her when I heard a loud thud. I called her name – "Kylie, Kylie!" – but she did not respond. As I rounded the corner of the bathroom, I saw her. There was my baby girl, crunched up in front of the bathtub between the toilet and a small cabinet. She was having a seizure — the kind you see in the movies where the entire body is jerking. Her eyes were open but she could not see me. Somehow her 90-pound frame seemed to weigh three hundred pounds as I tried with all my power to twist her into the doorway where I could at least have more room to panic. I was screaming. I am so grateful that she has amnesia when she has her seizures. I kept screaming for my son, Kaiden, to come and help me, but he too had been paralyzed by hearing my screams. I called 911 and somehow, I was able to give them my name and address and they came. By the time they arrived, Kylie's face was grey and there was a blue ring around her mouth. I could not think about anything except *Please don't die, please don't die!* All I could do was cry and cry. I cannot put into words the pain that I felt in that moment. I felt such betrayal from God, from Jay, from anyone and everyone that was not in pain in that moment. It does not have to make sense when grief consumes your very being. I felt like I had been through enough, I felt that Kylie had been through enough. What is enough? Somehow the rescue team came and they took her to Duke Emergency Department (ED). In the ED she did not have much of a workup – no EEG, maybe she had some blood tests, I am not sure. They sent us home without any medication and without a diagnosis.

Over the next few weeks Kylie had many tests, procedures, and more seizures. Suddenly, my little girl went from a healthy teenager to having an abnormal magnetic resonance imaging (MRI), electroencephalogram (EEG) and electrocardiogram (EKG) all in one week. I was paralyzed with fear that she would die. It was at this time that Kylie was diagnosed with Epilepsy. Eventually, I settled into the rhythm of giving medication to her each day at 6:30 a.m. and then again at 6:30 p.m. I was on a mission. Even when she played volleyball for her school, at 6:30 p.m. I would go onto the court and give her the medication that was meant to stop any seizures.

Kylie had many seizures over the next few years, and we had many medication changes during this time – always looking for the magic potion that would cure her epilepsy. In July of 2011 Kylie underwent 10 hours of craniofacial surgery to correct a birth defect that made her airway collapse on itself.

The surgery required that her mouth be wired shut for several weeks. She slowly recovered and returned to her normal life as she was, by then, in high school. In November of 2011 she had a seizure that was thought to have been brought on by an infection in her mouth. Her oral surgeon determined that it would be best to remove as many of the eight plates that had been previously inserted to stabilize her jaw during her surgery the summer before. The bones had all healed and the plates were not serving any purpose. It was thought that they could possibly be the cause of the chronic infections that she was experiencing in her mouth.

December 11, 2011, at around 5:30 in the evening, Kylie had two seizures, one after the other. This event occurred several weeks after six of the eight plates had been removed from her mouth. I immediately panicked. EMS arrived within three minutes, and they loaded her with valium to try and stop the seizure. While one of the EMTs attempted to get the stretcher up our steep front porch steps, the EMT who was inside assessing Kylie's condition decided that Kylie couldn't wait for the stretcher to be brought into the house. Instead, he quickly lifted her into his arms and ran to the ambulance. They immediately headed to Duke Children's Hospital. I followed in my car.

In the emergency room, doctors determined that she had an infection in one of the two remaining plates in her jaw. At that time, there was no critical care bed available for her, so we had to wait in the Emergency Department (ED). The neurologists had sedated Kylie so much that she was essentially in a coma. I sat in a chair by her bed and just held her hand while she slept. I felt so completely overwhelmed and alone. I felt powerless. The fear of losing my baby girl consumed me. Kylie was in the hospital for almost two weeks before being discharged. Her recovery was slow and she had to be homeschooled for several weeks until she was strong enough to go back to school. Since Kylie was 13 years old, I was already obsessed with keeping her safe. I was so focused on Kylie that I often lost sight of my other kids, even though most of them were on their own by that point. Still my laser beam focus on Kylie was not healthy for her or for me. Kylie rebelled every step of the way. Any child who has been sheltered by an overprotective mom is destined to act out in some way. Kylie had mastered the art of temper tantrums since she was about five years old. By the time she turned 13 years old, her behavior was out of control. She and I together were a volatile mix that was set for an explosion at any moment.

Unfortunately, it took a few more years for the explosion to occur. I finally learned the lesson that Kylie had been trying to teach me for most of her young life. She needed me, as her mother, to demonstrate to her that I believed in her ability to make good decisions and to make a life for herself. I could no longer try and control her behavior so that I could control the outcomes that would often come from her bad decisions. I had to show her that I trusted that she could handle whatever lesson was coming her way. The truth was that while I understood on an intellectual level that this was what Kylie needed me to do, I was going to have to fake it until I could make it. My deep truth was that I did not actually believe that she was capable of navigating young adulthood without me. I had so much to learn and trusting her enough to let her go was the single hardest thing that I have ever done as a parent. I was terrified that something horrible was going to happen if I stepped out of the picture, but I stepped away, somehow trusting, she would be okay.

Dr. Shefali Tsabary wrote an amazing book called *The Conscious Parent*. I found this book for the first time in 2012. In this book Dr. Tsabary states that children serve as mirrors of their parents' forgotten self. She also says that children function as ushers of the parents' development. When I got this book, I devoured it quickly. The words in the book resonated with me and they represented the way that I thought that I was already parenting. The way that I thought that I was parenting and the way that I was actually parenting were at times, miles apart! A few months passed and I read the book again and then on my third pass through the book, something finally clicked for me. This was when I finally understood what Kylie had been trying to teach me since she was a little girl – it was my job to let go of Kylie. It is never a child's job to let go of their parent.

In 2014, Kylie was away at college. I had little contact with her for the next several months. There were several events that had occurred over the previous summer that compelled me to distance myself from her. While we still got together as a family over the holidays, I refused to delve into the nuances of her life. It took me a really long time to trust my decision and let go of her. I knew that during this time her siblings were there for her, guiding and supporting her, while our relationship, as mother and daughter, necessitated change. Each and every day, Kylie was on my mind. I prayed for her safety and for the strength to let her go, trusting that she would be okay without me.

For a while, she quit coming home for weekend visits or holiday breaks from college. My heart physically ached for the loss of her in my life, but I trusted that I was doing what was best for her. Everything in my house reminded me of her. I had a small collection of various orchid plants throughout my home. I cherished my orchid collection and I often thought of how much Kylie always loved them when they were blooming. Her favorite was a deep purple orchid that I kept in our living room. One day that orchid bloomed after having a long dormant period without blooming and the blossoms made me think of her. I wrote her a short poem and sent it to her that day, along with a picture of the beautiful blossom.

Finally

Today my orchid finally bloomed, and I thought of you…
I have watched each day as this small plant has struggled to produce its first small sprout.
Just like my orchid, you have faced each day since your birth with great tenacity and spirit.
After shedding the first blossoms, this orchid sat dormant for a long time with seemingly no change.
Yet I knew, just like you, change and growth were always happening just below the surface. When you faced obstacles that seemed insurmountable, like my orchid, you broke through.
While the loss of you in my life has torn my heart open, it is a necessary opportunity for me to let you go. I have for far too long kept you close to protect both of us and now recognize that on your own you must be.
I can now sit back and watch as you face your journey with grace, love and a spirit of determination that will allow your life to unfold into a beautiful blossom.
Today my orchid bloomed and I thought of you…

During this time apart from each other, Kylie was forced to do a lot of growing up. I had always recognized my overprotective tendencies when it came to parenting Kylie. I also realized that this behavior was detrimental to Kylie's own development. She had not previously been forced to face the consequences of her behavior, because I was always there to shelter her. Eventually, Kylie was finally able to spread her wings and create her own identity. It took us several months apart for both of us to come out on the other side into our new relationship. I do regret that it took me so long to see that I was not doing my job as her parent. Kylie remained patient with me and gave me as many opportunities as it took for me to learn what she was teaching me.

Kylie is now a mother of two beautiful children and a stepmother to three more. Watching her mother her beautiful children is such a gift for me. Her children are blessed to have such a compassionate and loving mother.

All five of my children are now parents to their own children. Watching them navigate parenthood has been such a gift to me. When I hear my children say things to their children that I had once said to them as children, I am reminded of the circle of life. Even though I have made a lot of mistakes through the years, a lot of love was sown, and this love is what binds me to my children and to my grandchildren. I am forever theirs.

I have always visualized and defined myself as a "mother." Initially, I had no idea what it meant to be a mother. Now, I see my role as mother very differently. A mother has to constantly work hard on herself so that she is not driven by her ego when she interacts with her children. She must be present – really present – to mother a child. It has been such an honor to parent my children. It wasn't until they grew older that I understood that during all those times I believed I was in charge and worried about how to guide and teach each child through their experiences, it was actually they who were in control of their own destinies. They were being led by their inner guides, which permitted them to demonstrate to me, through their wants and needs, how to allow them to navigate their own lives and thus shape their own destiny. Parenting is so complex and yet so incredibly transparent. If we really listen to our children, they will tell us what they need and allow us the opportunity to parent them in the way that they need and deserve to be parented.

In the words of Dr. Shefali Tsabary, *"A certain child enters our life with its individual troubles, difficulties, stubbornness, and temperamental challenges in order to help us become aware of how much we have yet to grow. The reason this works is that our children are able to take us into the remnants of our emotional past and evoke deeply unconscious feelings. Consequently, to understand where our internal landscape needs to develop, we need look no further than our children's gaze."*

LESSON NINE

Relationships are a mirror for one's own true self

So many of my past relationships had convinced me that being alone would be best for me. However, once I began to understand that relationships are meant to teach me about myself, I began to see the value in every past relationship. After all, I had a lot to learn about so many different things and relationships were definitely at the top of my list! I have always understood that mapping out the path for learning the life lessons I hadn't grasped during my childhood and adolescence would be a steep challenge for me. Lacking a solid foundation for building any kind of relationship, I was truly a novice when it came to understanding the complexities of forming a genuine partnership with someone.

Over the years, I have felt a lot of guilt about the fact that I have been married to four different men! Knowing my full history, I now have compassion for these past decisions. All of my previous relationships taught me something about myself. I must admit that I frequently entered into relationships before taking the time to work on myself and fully comprehend what I had experienced in the previous ones. When you use a relationship to complete the brokenness inside of you then that relationship is doomed to fail because you will inevitably choose a partner with the same brokenness inside of them. Without a doubt the most important thing I have learned about relationships is that you have to do your own work to heal your own wounds so that when you enter into a relationship you bring your best, whole self to that partnership! Finally, I came to a point in my life where I no longer wanted to settle for a project. The decision to no longer settle was the result of understanding my previous patterns in past relationships. I no longer needed to be rescued; I learned to rescue myself. Finally, I felt that I was ready for a partner. I wanted someone who saw the world the same way that I did. I wanted someone who was searching for their highest authentic self the same way that I was searching for my own true self. After my decision to parent Kylie differently and allow her to make her own decisions and experience her own consequences, I decided to focus all my energy on healing the many wounds within myself that kept me locked in the same unhealthy patterns with relationships. It was during this time, in early 2015, when I wrote in my journal, a list of what I wanted in a relationship. Below is what I wrote:

1. Someone who is kind, loving, authentic, honest, and present
2. Someone who loves me
3. Someone who loves my children
4. Someone who is willing to do their own work and support me in mine

I wrote this list believing that it was completely attainable! However, I knew that I had to be patient. I recognize that there is a natural rhythm to life, and I decided to take my time and allow myself to be fully present in this new experience. During this time, I began to explore my past relationships so that I could be better prepared for the present.

When my divorce from Jay was finalized and after I moved to Memphis, I had a wonderful friend whom I dated for a few years. Shortly after moving to Memphis, I joined my brother, Knox, in a class to study *A Course in Miracles*. The class was taught by a professor from the University of Memphis. Simply put, *A Course in Miracles* teaches that there are two basic thought systems: one of perception and one of knowledge. It teaches us about the reality of truth and how to see and understand our connections to one another. This was the class where I met my friend. He was a man of deep insight, but again our relationship was destined to run its course as we were two wounded souls trying to heal ourselves while in a relationship with each other. As I later realized, healing is a task best undertaken alone. The teachings from my two years of studying *A Course in Miracles* provided me with the foundation that I needed to start my own healing journey.

At the time that we dated we were not in sync with each other. We were both newly divorced and I was in a place in my life where I felt that my focus had to stay on my children. Fast forward 15 years, I was in a totally different place, both spiritually and physically, and he decided that I was his soulmate. Go figure! Somehow, I had become somebody's soulmate when I was no longer their mate! Navigating relationships while having young children was always difficult for me to maneuver. I lived in Memphis for almost seven years and during that time this man, who became a trusted friend, was the only person that I dated. This relationship, quite truthfully, was a space holder for me during that time in my life. Nonetheless, he remains in my memory as a valuable friend who played an important role in my life and I am grateful that our paths crossed.

By the time I moved back to North Carolina in 2006, I had only two children left at home. Kaiden was going into his senior year of high school, and Kylie was going into the sixth grade.

The first relationship that I had after moving to North Carolina was with the choir director from the church that we joined. We had joined a Baptist Church in downtown Durham because the daughter of a dear friend from our Memphis church family had recommended it. It seemed to be a seamless transition from our Memphis church to this new church in Durham.

Things seemed to fall into place very quickly after we moved to North Carolina. My relationship with the choir director started soon after we joined our new church. He was coming out of a long-term relationship, which destined our relationship to be more of a rebound connection for him, rather than an actual relationship. However, at that time I did not have this level of understanding. After about a year, he broke up with me. However, he did contact me a few years after our relationship had ended to ask if I would be willing to try having a relationship with him again, but I declined. I was by that time in a totally different place in my life.

One day I was watching Oprah and she was talking to Elizabeth Gilbert, author of the book *Eat, Pray, Love*. Elizabeth explained that a soulmate is someone who reflects back to you those things that you need to work on to further your own growth. Both people in the "soulmate" category have to do this for each other and then, in turn, be invested in continuing their own growth as they grow together. She went on to explain that this type of relationship is sometimes so intense that your soulmate could come into your life, but then might need to leave after their work is done. In other words, there is no guarantee that this soulmate relationship is a "forever" relationship as it might just be a "for right now" relationship.

Everyone wants to meet their soulmate, their one true love. Unfortunately, the concept of a soulmate does not exist in the way that most of us have been taught. Most people think a soulmate is someone that makes them feel good about themselves, who has the same interests as them, and likes the same things, as them. Or maybe they think that a soulmate is someone they're meant to spend forever with. But when you look at the concept of soulmate through the lens of teacher, as someone who challenges you to become someone greater than you were when you met them, then my ex-husband Jay was not only my greatest teacher, but he was also my soulmate. There was no other relationship that challenged me the way that one did and there was no other relationship that transformed me like that one did. I am forever grateful to Jay for his role in allowing me to become the kind of mother to our children that I wanted to be and mistakenly thought I already was. The connection that a mother has with her children is the single most important bond that a mother can have.

Unfortunately, when looking for a relationship with a partner, there are so many hidden obstacles that hinder one's ability to choose wisely. I did not date much at all for the first seven years after my divorce, except for my friend in Memphis, whom I dated on and off for about five years. Then when I moved to North Carolina in 2006, I was suddenly aware of every single man that was around me. I began dating almost instantly. After a year, I broke up with the choir director at my church, and I was suddenly back at square one, again. However, about a month after we broke up, I went to a birthday party that my brother was giving for my nephew who was turning 30 years old. At the party, I was sitting on the couch with my daughter, Kylie, when I saw two men walk in, heading straight toward my brother, Keith. Immediately, I recognized one of the men as the man who had come to me in a dream several years earlier.

In 2002, I went to Las Vegas for work and I took with me my best friend and then employee, Sheila. The first afternoon that we arrived, I decided to take a nap, while Sheila went to mingle with some of our colleagues' downstairs. While I was asleep, I had a very vivid dream about a man. He was standing in front of me wearing jeans, white tennis shoes and a red plaid flannel shirt with long sleeves that were rolled up to below his elbows. He had one hand in his pocket and he had an incredible smile. He had a head full of salt-and-pepper curly hair and striking crystal blue eyes that were gazing directly at me. I heard a voice say, "Kim, don't worry about finding someone who loves you because you will soon meet this man. His name is Scott."

I immediately woke up from my dream and ran downstairs to find Sheila. I was so excited to tell her about my dream. She listened intently and, better yet, she truly believed everything that I was telling her. For the next several years, Sheila would often ask me when I thought that I would finally be meeting Scott. Time passed, but I never felt anxious about when it would happen. I felt certain that eventually, Scott would find his way into my life.

Fast forward almost four years. I was at my nephew's party and in walks Scott! It is a truly powerful experience when you see your dream come to fruition right before your eyes. It was the same man that I had seen in that dream. I recognized him instantly and I immediately got up to go over and introduce myself. Typically, I am a very shy person and I would never describe myself as the kind of person to walk over to a stranger and introduce myself, but this time was different. In that moment I felt like I already knew Scott. Scott was busy talking to my brother, but I simply stepped in front of my brother, stuck out my hand and said, "Hi, I'm Keith's sister, Kim." He immediately leaned toward me, took my hand, looked me in the eyes, smiled and said, "Hi, I'm Scott!"

"Hi, I'm Scott!" I thought I was going to scream. It is hard not to scream when you are totally immersed in the presence of a miracle. The attraction between us was palpable, especially for me. The rest of the evening, we kept an eye on each other and talked several times before heading our separate ways. He gave me his business card before he left the party. The first person that I called when I got back home that evening was my dear friend, Sheila. We were both screaming with delight on the phone. She was thrilled that finally, Scott had made his way into my life! I emailed Scott after I got off the phone with Sheila. I did not hear back from him all day on Sunday, but then early Monday morning I got a reply. I could barely contain my excitement. He explained that he hadn't seen my email from Saturday because he didn't have access to his work email until he returned to the office on Monday morning. He told me that he had spent Sunday trying to figure out how he could get my contact information from my brother, so he could call me. Two days later, we had our first official date. I was so consumed with the whole miracle situation that I even told him about "The Dream." I referred to it as "The Dream" because this event became such a significant part of my life that it consumed me for the next seven years. However, when our on-again-off-again relationship broke up permanently, I was devastated. It took me a long time and a lot of therapy to come to terms with the meaning behind "The Dream." Was it real? What did it mean? What lesson was I supposed to learn? Was it really from God?

This is what I know to be true: It *was* real. It meant that God is watching over me and I must learn to trust myself and trust my relationship with God. So, if this is true, then what happened to Scott? Well, I learned that everyone has free will. I truly believe that Scott and I were in love, but he was not in a place where he could accept the love that I had for him. He would often tell me that he felt so undeserving of the love that I had for him. After several years, when we ultimately ended our relationship for good, we both acknowledged that the love we had for each other was genuine and sufficient for the time we spent together. For the first time in my life, I could honestly say that I knew true, mutual, transparent love. Maybe if circumstances had been different for Scott at the time that we met, our relationship would have had a different outcome. Nonetheless, I learned what true love felt like and when it would come to me again, I knew I would recognize its presence. I had learned to trust myself. All in all, it was one of the most magical times of my life and even though the outcome was not what I would have wanted, I have no regrets! To see my dream come to fruition was a once in a lifetime experience and it demonstrated to me to always leave room in my life for miracles!

Finding someone who is willing and able to stay is where I found myself over and over again. What makes a man stay? At times, this seemed to be an unanswered question for me. Sometimes I thought that maybe it was me. Maybe I was the one who couldn't stay? Maybe all my issues with the men that I dated had really been about me and not about them. Maybe my relationship with Jay was the only real relationship where I was prepared to stay, and the irony was that he could not. I have thought about these same questions many times throughout my life. Eventually I came to understand that, of course, it is about me! My past relationships offered me the opportunity to recognize this truth – relationships are mirrors to our true self!

My upbringing did not prepare me to have a healthy, loving relationship. The only consistent male in my family was my maternal grandfather, Gramps. Gramps and Grams were one of the only couples in my family who married and stayed together until they died, both in their 90s. My grandfather was definitely submissive to my grandmother, who seemed to be the one in charge. My Gramps was softer and easier to talk to when I was young. He was a kind and loving man.

Aside from my cousins' dad, Earl, whom we lived with for about a year before relocating to what would become my hometown in West Virginia, I had no other stable male role models in my early life. While not having a constant male role model in my life was difficult for me, I always assumed that this reality of my childhood was hardest for my three younger brothers. Maybe it was just as hard on all of us, for different reasons.

I had to learn the hard way how to navigate relationships. Initially, the only way I knew how to pick a mate was based on physical appearance. If they looked handsome, then I assumed that I could mold them into what I needed them to be. This was my thinking pattern when I married my first husband. Obviously, I had not been around domestic violence. I knew that I could sometimes hear my mom crying when my dad and her would "talk" in a room separate from us kids. But I never saw with my own eyes or felt the terror of domestic violence until I married my first husband. I always imagined myself as someone who could defend herself, but the reality is that I was no match for my husband's fury or his violence towards me.

After a relationship ends with a violent partner, you understand the answer to everyone's question of "Why didn't she just leave him?" She didn't leave him because she couldn't leave him. Unless you have experienced domestic violence, you cannot understand what it does to your psyche. When your spirit has been broken from exposure to domestic abuse, you lose your sense of self, making it impossible to rescue yourself.

I was 20 years old when I met Jay. Twenty sounds like the correct age to be an adult, but, for me, it was not. I think Jay and I both lacked maturities. Jay had grown up with one older sister and he was definitely raised by his parents to be successful. He was the golden child in his family. His destiny was determined for him when he was very young; he was raised to become a doctor. This dream would satisfy his mother's vision for herself that she was an exceptional mother with an exceptional son. I can remember when we first got together and Jay shared with me his dream of becoming a travel agent. Back in the late 1970s, travel arrangements were made by a travel agent. The agent frequently traveled to various locations around the world to become familiar with the accommodations and available vacation activities for their clients. This was Jay's dream job! But he knew that instead he would become a doctor to make his parents, mostly his mother, happy. This was Jay's life script. I believe that his decision to pick up the life script that was prepared for him by his parents helped lead him to his secret life, which he subsequently hid from us, his own family. Looking back over our relationship, it is easy to see that we were destined to end our relationship in divorce because neither of us were mature enough, or had the courage when we married, to write our own life scripts.

After moving to North Carolina in 2006, I became a member on an online dating service called eHarmony. I remained active, on and off, for several years. It helped me go out on a lot of first dates, but second and third dates were rare. The chatter in my mind was that I just wanted to stay home and isolate, whenever I wasn't working. Dating became a way for me to continue to keep pushing myself forward, out into the world, and outside the safety of my home.

eHarmony was where I met my current husband, Geno. Even though we were married less than a month after we had our first in-person meeting, neither of us have any regrets for our hasty decision. Any relationship will show you your true self and if you are unable or unwilling to see that, then the relationship will be doomed to fail. The key is to understand this element of relationships and be committed to learning what you need to learn about yourself in order to grow together as a couple!

I had spent so much of my adult life in therapy and I was determined to heal all of my childhood issues and bring my best self into my relationship with Geno. Even though this was my intention, I have continued to learn about myself throughout our marriage. Our early disagreements almost always centered around my work and my children. These were our two major trigger points as a married couple. I will admit that these two issues were very sensitive topics for me and I had a lot to learn about myself through my relationship with Geno. Most importantly, I had to learn to trust him.

I was recruited by Duke University in 2006 from the University of Tennessee. I was so excited about my move back to North Carolina, since my two oldest children were in college in North Carolina! My work at Duke was so important to me and over the first few years that I was employed I was able to build a successful research program that was not only financially solvent (when your assets outweigh your anticipated debt) but was also viewed as a key stakeholder for the Department of Pediatrics. I loved my job and for many years I would often work 60 to 70 hours a week and still cover our after-hours pager over the weekend. The pager allowed parents of our research patients, providers, and anyone else to contact me 24 hours a day and seven days a week. I was devoted to my job and to my staff. This type of work schedule left little room for a relationship.

Geno had been retired for many years prior to us meeting. He had been living in Central America since his retirement in 1999 and had returned to the United States, full time, in 2014, one year prior to our meeting. By this time, his children were all adults and living on their own. During his time in Costa Rica, he worked for several years for a US-owned company that owned several thousand hectares (a metric unit that is larger than an acre: 1 hectare is approximately 2.47 acres) on the Pacific Coast. He also purchased several acres of land on his own and spent his time developing the infrastructures for these properties. The skillsets that he developed during his time in Costa Rica became a great resource for us each and every time we have sold or purchased a home in North Carolina.

Eventually after my children had all graduated from college and moved forward with their own adult lives, my identity as a mother changed. Suddenly, my identity was tied directly to my job at Duke University. I was no longer in an active mothering role and therefore, my identity became Director of the Neonatal Perinatal Research Unit for the division of Neonatology. My work/life balance became even more skewed during this time in my life.

When Geno and I married in 2015, I told him that I would work for an additional five more years before retiring. I ended up working much longer. I did not retire until May 15, 2024, after much persuasion from Geno. I had worked five years more than what I had initially told Geno. He deserved for me to retire; I deserved for me to retire.

He had spent much of our married life with me working excessively, and while I can see that now, I was often defensive and protective of my work schedule at the time. This led to many unnecessary disagreements and tensions in our marriage. Although I can recognize this truth clearly now, I resisted accepting it for years.

I also had a real chip on my shoulder when it came to my children. I was like a fierce mama bear, always ready to protect her cubs, even though they were all grown adults by the time we married and no longer required my protecting. Geno had three grown children of his own and three grown grandchildren. I had five children and fourteen grandchildren, of which, six were born after Geno and I married in 2015. My children had always been my entire life. My role as their mother had always been the greatest gift of my life. My kids were used to my being available if and when they needed me. I admit that I had set things up this way because I felt that this kept me connected to them. Some might say that this type of relationship would keep my children dependent on me, which might, also, be true. Some would also see this close relationship as unhealthy. At the beginning of my marriage to Geno, I still had a lot to learn about parenting my adult children.

This type of relationship with grown children was certainly not a concept that was familiar to Geno. He often questioned me about the lack of balance that I had related to my children and the dependencies that Geno felt existed within my immediate family. He often saw my children as an obstacle to our happiness. It was not my children's fault. It was due to my dependence on them. Once again, it took me some time to learn how to navigate the challenges of parenting my adult children while also bonding with my beautiful grandchildren. His children were spread out over the country and despite being very close, they did not get together very often. Me and my kids were used to frequent gatherings such as holidays and birthdays for the grandchildren. Geno was not used to having so many family gatherings, and this provided ample opportunity for misunderstandings to occur in our marriage.

Geno had been fortunate to have the opportunity when he was a young teenager to spend his eighth-grade summer traveling with four of his best friends and one chaperone across the United States and up through Alaska and past the Artic Circle. This experience had a life-changing impact on the trajectory of his life. For a kid from a small rural town in Connecticut, this trip opened his eyes to an amazing world, as he experienced new people and adventures. I knew when we married, that Geno was a man who loved to travel and was comfortable getting in his truck and driving across the country to California, often without a plan. This was not something I felt very comfortable doing, especially considering that I would have needed to take several weeks off from work, which seemed impossible to me at the time. Geno made two such trips across the country during the first few years of our marriage. At that time, I could not understand his desire to do this and I took it personally, which caused even more problems in our marriage. To me, Geno was a restless spirit who didn't appear to be content staying in one place for too long. When he lived in Central America, he kept a rental house in Oregon for when he would visit the States for several months each year. I cherished owning my own home and I was more comfortable at home than anywhere else. All of these differences quickly became opportunities for disharmony to arise in our marriage. However, they also provided us with the chance to learn about one another and, ultimately, discover how to build our relationship together.

So much about my relationship with Geno has at times been hard and yet the good parts have provided me with joy beyond what I could have ever imagined. I see him clearly and he sees me clearly. I will admit that when we first married, I did not feel like he was able to see himself clearly. I probably didn't always, consistently, see myself clearly, either. Geno grew up in a home with two older brothers and a younger sister. His oldest brother lived full time with his maternal grandparents and only visited during the summer months when he was out of school. Geno's loving mother was an attentive woman who was a gifted artist. His dad served in the war (World War II) and could not handle any level of stress, which would result in an explosive temper that made Geno's childhood one of great trepidation. Geno later learned as an adult that his dad had been part of the Office of Strategic Services (OSS) during the war. His dad had been recruited as a young man because he was a paratrooper who was also fluent in Italian. The OSS was the precursor to the current Central Intelligence Agency (CIA). Geno did not see his childhood home as a safe space and he spent as much time as he could outside the home. While living at home with his parents, Geno's outlet was playing sports. His athletic ability provided him with a lot of stability, self-confidence and attention from his peers and teachers. Learning more about his father's life helped him understand his father's behaviors when he was a child. We both recognize and appreciate that understanding the truths of your childhood can significantly influence your adult relationships. These experiences play a crucial role in shaping your identity as an adult.

Geno left home at 18 years of age and he rarely looked back, except to see and care for his mother during her later years. Geno had a 30-year marriage to the mother of two of his children. His siblings grew distant from each other as time passed. Fast forward to 2015, Geno met and married me, a woman with lots of kids, grandchildren, and a tight network of four siblings. When we first married, Geno kept most of his feelings and emotions hidden. I, on the other hand, am a highly sensitive and emotional person. I am sure there were times that he wondered if this union could possibly work!

I can honestly say that through it all, it was all worth it! Geno is my person. He is the one that I am meant to be with. He gets me and I get him. It took us both a long time to understand each other and see that we had both been given the opportunity to learn about ourselves and each other through our relationship. We both realized that these opportunities were some of life's gifts that we had both been missing. We have a connection that transcends words. Our union has allowed both of us to grow both individually and as a couple. He is my reward at the end of my journey and he was well worth the wait. We talk often about different milestones in our lives to see if perhaps we had crossed paths sometime previously. I trust this man completely and he trusts me. Everything that I have learned throughout my life about relationships, the therapy that I had, the amazing angels who helped me along my path, and my own determination to heal, brought me here, to this wonderful, amazing, and most handsome man, my husband. I am eternally grateful!

Relationships are a mirror to our own true self. There is no greater teacher than what is provided to us by being in a relationship. Relationships will strip away all of the pretenses that we have built up around ourselves throughout the years. The key to any successful relationship is a willingness to look within yourself first, before placing blame or accusations at your partner. If you want to be in a successful relationship, you have to be willing to see who you really are and if that is not someone that you want to be, you have to be brave enough to make a change.

LESSON TEN

Life is a precious gift

The ability to experience life to the fullest is a gift. It has taken me a long time to understand, recognize and accept the many gifts that have come to me in my life. Fortunately for me, life was patient and provided the necessary opportunities for me to recognize what had always been right in front of me. Through the veils of darkness, there are often miracles sprinkled in, if we allow ourselves to see them.

One such miracle in my life occurred when I made the decision to move to Memphis, Tennessee, after my divorce from Jay. Moving to Memphis was a monumental decision for me. Moving my family from the safety and security that I thought that I had with Jay, was my greatest test. How could I successfully parent my children without him? I had absolutely no confidence left inside of me as I stepped off the ledge, trusting that I would learn to fly, and made my way to Memphis. My brother, Knox, helped me by connecting me with a local realtor. In February of 1999, I made plans to fly to Memphis to meet with the realtor so that I could find a house for my family. Before heading to Memphis, I had a telephone conversation with the realtor, Barbara, to discuss the type of house we would need. I told her that I needed a minimum of five bedrooms with at least three full bathrooms. I also told her that I was hoping to find a large house with an in-ground pool. I wanted to stay within the city limits of Memphis, even though I did not have a job lined up, initially. I flew into Memphis on a Wednesday night and spent the next two days viewing the available homes for sale in the area. On Friday afternoon, Barbara drove me by a large historic home located at 1401 Goodbar Avenue. She told me that the couple selling the home had recently had an open house and that they had received an offer for $369,000. The owners had been given one week to accept or reject the current offer. Barbara offered to call the owners to see if they would be willing to let me view the house if I was interested. Barbara knew that the house was above my price range, but it had everything that I was looking for, including an in-ground pool. Barbara contacted the owners and they agreed to let me see their house that afternoon! As soon as I went inside the front door, I knew it was the house for us. It was a two-story house with six bedrooms, three bathrooms, an in-ground pool and a carriage house that was currently being used as a rental property. It is hard to describe the hope that I felt as I walked through the house that day. At that time, my divorce had been more than three years in the making. As I walked through that house, I felt like I had been running a marathon, just trying to make it to the finish line. For me that finish line would be moving myself and my children to our new home in Memphis and I needed to believe that this was going to be our house.

The offer that the couple had previously accepted was based on the contingency that the family making the offer could sell their current home. The couple that owned the Goodbar house were currently building a new home in the suburbs of Memphis. They told my realtor, Barbara, that they would be willing to accept another offer only if the offer came without a contingency attached. They had to make a decision on their current offer by Sunday at noon. I told Barbara that I would have to go home and think about my next step, since the house was outside of my price point. I flew back to North Carolina that Friday evening.

That night, the decision of whether or not to make an offer on the house was weighing heavily on my mind. I knew that I had less than two days to make a decision. I typically spend a lot of time in prayer and mindful thought before going to sleep each night and that Friday night was no exception. For me, it was not that I was looking for an answer, but I was looking for peace about my decision to move my family to Memphis. During the night, I felt God was telling me to move forward with an offer on the house and I felt guided to make an offer of $319,000. I woke the next morning, and I was filled with hope for the first time in a very long time. I was so excited to call my realtor and tell her about my dream.

I headed to work. I called Barbara on Saturday morning from my office at the hospital. At that time, I was working as a lactation consultant at Carolinas Medical Center in Charlotte, North Carolina. I eagerly relayed the details of my dream to Barbara, along with my offer to purchase the home. I paused for her response. She was silent for a few moments and then she tentatively said, "Are you sure you want to offer $319,000? You are aware that the current offer they have on the table is for $369,000 and that their original asking price was $375,000." I confirmed that this was my understanding as well. She then said, "What if we change the offer to at least $330,000 or even $335,000?" I declined her suggestion. I again confirmed that I believed that I needed to make my offer for $319,000. Barbara agreed to follow my request, but she did so with many reservations.

It was hard for me to explain to people but throughout my life I have had times of immense "knowing." I have always felt a connection to a higher power that I refer to as God. These periods of "knowing" have always been of great comfort to me, but I do understand that some people may not understand my experiences with these events. I relayed the events of my dream to my realtor exactly as they had been revealed to me the previous night. I could sense her hesitation in knowing how to respond back to me after I recounted my experience to her.

After talking to Barbara on the phone, I continued to work through my patient list for that day. Around two in the afternoon, I received a page from Barbara, and I made my way back to my office to give her a call. With great anticipation, I dialed the phone. Barbara answered the phone on the first ring. She quickly blurted out, "Kim, you are not going to believe this, but they have accepted your offer. The house is yours!" I literally fell to my knees, in my office, in tears. Even though I had faith that I was making the offer that I was given in my dream, I still could not believe that it was real. I had finally found a house for my family. I was filled with so much gratitude! I began to believe that this move was the right move for us.

As it turned out, the owners of the Goodbar house were facing a huge invoice from their contractor for their new house in the suburbs. The contingency attached to the first offer was something that the Goodbar owners didn't want to gamble on and so they decided to accept my much lower bid! A miracle had touched my family and I was so very grateful. In the end, the necessary steps to close the purchase on the Memphis house were impeded by a delay in the divorce process from Jay. My realtor worked out a deal with the mortgage lender who allowed me to rent my home until the divorce could be finalized, which took an additional two months. After that, the mortgage loan was processed and the house was ours!

Our home on Goodbar Street marked the start of our new family unit—just my children and me. Many missteps in my life had brought me to that moment, and each experience taught me valuable lessons that helped me move forward for both myself and my family.

Buying and moving into our dream home in Memphis was another exercise in waiting. My whole life has been spent waiting. Waiting for someone to make me feel safe. Waiting for someone to recognize the lost, frightened, naïve girl who existed inside of me. Waiting for someone to love me. Even in a crowd of siblings and at times two parents, I always felt alone. I could never understand why the rest of my family seemed so unaware of the impending doom that I could see each and every day throughout my childhood. Doom did not necessarily have a name or any type of distinction, but it was still very real to me. Doom made the possibility of any light coming into my life seem almost impossible. I accepted this as my life. I did not know any other way of being except in this perpetual place of fear.

This was the 18-year-old girl who met and married a man who would later prove himself to be just that – doom. After a 16-month marriage to him, I found myself alone – yet again. Each and every day seemed to be such a struggle. I had my eating disorder for company, which I wore as a coat of armor around my heart. And then, less than three years after my first divorce, I met and later married the father of my children. I have explored every crack and crevice of that relationship and I am constantly reminded that Jay, too, was just a scared boy who married a scared girl. Together we tried to make a marriage but neither of us knew how. After our youngest daughter, Kylie, turned one, and the reality of the secret life that he masked himself with was finally removed, we could no longer pretend that we had a marriage worth fighting for.

In 2006, after having lived in Memphis for seven years, I made the decision to move yet again. My career as faculty with the University of Memphis, School of Medicine, was at a turning point and I felt ready to move on. At that time both of my two oldest children had moved back to North Carolina for college, Karson was in College at the University of Memphis and my two youngest were still living at home with me. The question was where should we move? On March 24, 2006, I had one of those dreams that guided me forward. I felt God telling me that it was time to move home and that I was to begin to prepare to go home that very summer. Home, to me, was always North Carolina. I told my children the following day that we were moving back to North Carolina. They were both surprised but they, too, were ready to move back home.

I had a wonderful church family in Memphis that included a group of women who had nurtured and supported me since I moved there in 1999. There were three older women who taught my Sunday School class (small group of women who meet to focus on spiritual growth and community building) that became like mothers to me. Their names were Martha, Margaret, and Helen. These three women were amazing! They loved me and my children and their support meant the world to me. I told my Sunday school class on Sunday, March 26, 2006, that I would be moving that summer to return home to North Carolina. Martha and Margaret were teaching the class that day and they were both startled by this news. They immediately began to pepper me with questions: "Where are you going to work? Where are you going to live? What prompted such a drastic decision?" I told them about my dream. They both felt that I was being too hasty and they cautioned me to slow things down before jumping into such a big life change, so quickly. I knew that they were worried about me and, more importantly, I knew how much they cared about me and my family, but I assured them that I felt confident that this was God's plan for me and my family. So, I began to prepare to move back to North Carolina.

I called a moving company the next day to reserve a truck for July of 2006. When the company asked me for the destination city for the upcoming move, I told them that I did not yet know the answer to that question. I assured them that I would have that information for them at least one month prior to the scheduled moving date. I immediately started looking for jobs at North Carolina universities. I was not at all sure what type of job I wanted to do. Did I want to stay in academic research or return to graduate teaching? In the following weeks, I attended several interviews at various universities in North Carolina and even applied for a head research position at Children's National Hospital in Washington, D.C. At first, I was eager to secure a job quickly, even if it wasn't specifically in North Carolina. I figured that as long as it was nearby, like in Washington, it would suffice. I began to pack up our home to prepare for the upcoming move. After my initial interview with the hospital in DC, and subsequent notification that I had been moved to the second round of interviews that included only two remaining candidates, I made the decision to remove my candidacy from consideration. I knew that I had to trust in my decision to move back to North Carolina. Close to North Carolina was not good enough and I had to trust the process that was slowly unfolding before me. So, I did. Somehow, I would make my way back to North Carolina.

Two weeks later, on my day off, I got a call from my friend, employee, and nurse manager for my staff, Sheila, at the University of Tennessee. She told me that someone from Duke University had called my office phone looking for me and they left a number for me to return their call. I had no idea who would be calling me from Duke, but I promptly called the number. The number was for the cell phone of the head of the Division of Neonatology at Duke University, the Division Chief! He answered the phone and told me that he had recently been to a meeting in Washington, DC, with a friend of mine who was a general surgeon with the University of Tennessee, School of Medicine. This surgeon and I had worked closely together over the previous few years trying to get one of his big research projects funded, and we were eventually successful, despite encountering multiple obstacles along the way. Apparently, my friend had discussed with him the many hurdles that we had faced with our Memphis project and how we had eventually procured funding for the project. This division chief was facing many of the same issues with his entire research program and he asked me if I would be willing to come to Durham for an interview! This call occurred on a Tuesday, and I flew to Durham the following week for two days of interviews.

I was convinced that this was my job, even before my initial meeting with the Division Chief, on Day 1. I had two full days of interviews with different faculty members. I ended the second day of interviews with another meeting with the Division Chief. I told him at that time that I was meant for this job and that I was very confident that I could turn his research program around and make it financially solvent, ensuring that the assets for the division would far exceed the projected debt within five years. He jokingly said, "It sounds like you're telling me that you have the moving truck outside!" I responded, "No it's not outside yet, but it will be soon!" I was never as confident in a job interview as I was with this one. Well, I got the job! I founded the Neonatal Perinatal Research Unit (NPRU) and spend the next 19 years building and sustaining the NPRU, which currently serves as the professional infrastructure and clinical expertise directed toward improving the quality of care and long-term outcomes for critically ill newborns at Duke University. I actually got a job at Duke University without ever having applied for a job!

My first day of work was August 1, 2006. I remember walking onto campus that day. It was a bright and sunny day. As I walked from the parking garage to my then, new office, located in the Bell Research Building at Duke University, I was filled with emotion. I had been born in Durham and my family had moved away when I was just an infant. My dad had been a law student at Duke University and he had passed away in October of 1999, just a few short months after I had moved my family to Memphis, Tennessee. I felt a sudden connection that linked me somehow with the father that I barely even knew. My father had chosen to go to law school at Duke, despite also being accepted by both Harvard and Princeton, and now Duke had recruited and chosen me to come back to the same place where I had started. I was forever grateful for God's hand in my life. Another miracle had touched my life.

One tidbit about my friend and then employee, Sheila. In 2006, I was recruited by Duke University and became the Operational Research Director for the division of Neonatology. As part of my hiring package, I was able to bring Sheila with me to Durham, North Carolina. Sheila had served as the nurse manager for my staff at Le Bonheur Children's Hospital in Memphis and when she moved to Durham she maintained her role as nurse manager for my staff at Duke. Sheila helped me establish the Neonatal Perinatal Research Unit for the University. She stayed with me for five years before heading back to Memphis, Tennessee. She was a true blessing in my life and I am forever grateful that our paths crossed in this lifetime. All these years later, she remains a precious friend to me and to my family!

For the next 10-plus years I saturated my life with my children and my work. I always knew that eventually I would marry again but I also knew that in order to attract the kind of man that I wanted, that I would first have to do the work to heal the wounds that had left me so scarred, and that is what I did. I had one goal: to find someone who could love me the same way that I love – all in! Navigating the path to this goal has been a journey. When people say that life is about the journey and not the destination, that is so true. Without the struggles, obstacles, triumphs, lessons, bridges, friends, and faith in a higher power, I would not be where I am today. Today I am happily married to a man who I recognized immediately as the one for me. I know that it is such a cliché when people say that they have met their person who they are meant to be with – but then it actually happened to me and in that moment, we were both in a place of awareness that allowed us to recognize each other.

It happened on September 13, 2015. I was in Hickory, North Carolina, visiting my grandchildren for the weekend. Geno and I had connected through an internet dating site and we had been emailing each other for several weeks. Eventually the geographical distance between us seemed too much to navigate for him and he put our communication on hold. A few months later, I reached out to him again when I knew that I would be visiting my family, who lived an hour away from where Geno lived. I asked if he would like to meet before I headed back to Durham. He accepted and so we set a date. We were going to meet on September 13, 2015, at two in the afternoon, for dessert at the Bob Evans Restaurant off Exit 126.

My sister and my mom had come to my son Karter's house to watch some of his children for a few days while he and his wife went out of town. I had agreed to meet my mom and sister there for the weekend to ensure that they had what they needed to successfully get the kids to and from school during the upcoming week. On Sunday morning my mother and sister got up early and took my granddaughter to meet up with my niece and her son about an hour away in Charlotte, North Carolina. They left before noon, and I kept questioning the need to stay an additional two hours until I was scheduled to meet Geno. I considered just sending him a text and canceling our plans because I knew that I could be back home in Durham in two hours. While I scurried around the house packing up my things and assuring myself that I should just go on back home early, suddenly my phone rang. It was my oldest grandson, Bryson. He had gone to spend the night with his other grandparents the night before. "Would you come and pick me up and take me to get some lunch and then bring me back to Maw maw's house?" Bryson asked me.

I immediately said, "Yes, of course!" I was just getting ready to leave his parents' house and I assured him that I would be by to pick him up soon. I didn't think about the time. At that point I was convinced that after getting lunch with Bryson and then returning him back to his other grandparents, I would simply send an apology text to Geno and let him know that I was heading back home early instead of staying to meet with him. My grandson chose to go eat at the mall, which took us a little longer than I had planned. After getting our food, he proceeded to sit and talk to me about things that were happening in his 13-year-old life. It had been a long time since we had enjoyed private time together, just talking. At that time, Bryson had three younger siblings and it was rare for me to have much individual time with any of grandchildren. I quickly became immersed in our conversation together and the time sped past us.

Just as suddenly and as unexpected as Bryson's call to have lunch with him had come, so too was his response that he was ready to go back to his Maw maw's house. It was 1:40 PM. By the time I took him back to his grandparents, and returned to Exit 126, it was exactly 2:00 PM. I stayed to meet Geno. There are moments of synchronicity in one's life that are hard to miss and this was definitely one of those times.

I sent a text to Geno telling him I was on my way. I turned to pull into the parking lot and I could feel the many butterflies fluttering in my stomach. I parked my car and sent Geno a text stating that I had just arrived. He responded that he too had arrived. I had no idea what kind of car he was driving or even what he looked like. I had only seen the few pictures that he had posted of himself on the eHarmony website. I took a deep breath and got out of my car. I started walking towards the front door of the restaurant when I saw a tall, sexy man with gray curly hair and sunglasses coming towards me from the opposite side of the parking lot – it was Geno. I recognized him from the pictures that he had posted on the dating site but he was so much more handsome and younger looking in person! We quickly greeted each other with a smile and a huge hug and then we went inside. We were seated almost immediately, as we were in between the lunch and dinner crowds.

We both slipped into opposite sides of the booth and immediately fell into deep conversation. Our conversations were deep, spiritual, and often times, they evoked feelings of vulnerability inside of me. Geno would later tell me that for him he had never had this level of spiritual understanding with someone. He felt that we were of one mind! I had often thought about the man that I was looking for and I felt that I was clear in my mind about what I was looking for, but this man was so much more than I could ever have imagined. We talked for almost three hours, and then I told him that I needed to get back home because I had a long drive ahead of me followed by work early the next morning. After paying our bill, we chatted as we walked towards the front door. However, my mind was racing with ideas on how I could find a way to ensure that I would see him again. We both hugged each other longer than normal and Geno later told me that he had tried to kiss me but that I turned my head. He joked about getting the forearm shiver (which is a football technique to keep an opponent away [something that he had to later explain to me as I was unfamiliar with the reference]) when he tried to kiss me. I was unaware of his attempt to kiss me when we parted. As we separated and I made my way to the car, again my mind was swirling with ideas of how I was going to see this man again. I sent him a text as I was leaving, telling him that I had a wonderful time and that I hoped we could see each other again, and he responded quickly. As soon as I arrived back home, we continued our conversations via email. He always replied right away. The next day, when I got home from work there was a package on my porch from Geno! I was thrilled. He had ordered two of his favorite books for me on past lives by author, Brian Weiss. Weiss' books embody the awareness that there is nothing to fear because we are all connected, our souls are eternal, and love is real! I immediately sent Geno an email thanking him for the books. I devoured the books, reading both of them in less than a week. I had actually ordered two books for Geno after arriving home from our first meeting on Sunday. His books from me arrived the following day, on Monday. Neither of us knew that we had both sent each other copies of our favorite books! Again, another example of synchronicity had touched us both!

I wanted to know everything that I could about this man because I knew within a few days that I was falling hard for him.

Geno told me that he loved me first, but I was already thinking it myself! We agreed that he would come to spend some time with me on the 20th of September, exactly seven days after our first in-person meeting. We were both very anxious for the 20th to arrive and we spent a lot of time emailing, texting, and talking on the phone. Neither of us knew what was happening but we knew that it was real, and we were both excited to see where the relationship was going to take us.

September 20th was a Sunday, and Geno arrived in the middle of the afternoon. I was waiting outside on my tiny porch peering down the street for the sight of his bright red truck. I was so very excited. I had not told anyone about him – he was my little secret. In some ways I did not want to let anyone else into our circle, and in other ways I was a little embarrassed about how fast I had fallen for this man that I secretly hoped would not hurt me.

Finally, he arrived, and as I stood on the top step of my porch, we hugged each other for an extra-long time. We then went inside my house. A few steps inside the door, he kissed me for the first time. We had fallen in love with each other, and we had never even kissed. It was so very special to me. I had scheduled a few days off work so that I could spend time with him, uninterrupted. That night when we went to bed together, we made love, and even though we were both nervous we both knew that this was something, really, really, special.

Navigating any relationship with me is not without obstacles. I am very emotional and I am not able to hide my emotions for very long. The certainty that I had around Geno was quickly replaced with doubt as I felt an overwhelming sense of fear consume my being. Fear that he would not love me enough, fear that he would leave me, fear that he would not love my children the way that I needed him to love them. The fear began to consume me. After Geno fell asleep that night, I got up and went into my daughter's room to sleep. I did not feel comfortable sleeping with him – this is what fear does to me. I began to second guess every decision that I had made since I met Geno. I heard him wake up early and carry some stuff down the stairs and I assumed that he was sneaking out of my house to go back home – this is how my mind works.

I laid in bed crying and visited all the moments in my head where I knew that I had made the wrong decision with Geno. Granted we had not had very many moments together since we had only just met each other nine days prior. I got out of bed after a little while and went downstairs and that's when I realized that his truck was still parked in front of my house, but his bike was missing from his bike rack – he had simply gone for a bike ride! I was both thrilled and surprised. When he got back to my house from his morning bike ride, we talked for a long time, and he asked me why I had not slept with him the night before. I shared with him how the reality of a possible relationship filled me with fear. Suddenly, I began to scroll through all of the broken relationships that I had experienced throughout my life. Could this be real? What if my heart got broken again? We talked for a few hours and as I expressed my fears and hesitations, he listened with a calmness and a knowing that I did not fully understand. Finally, my fears began to melt away and I started to trust him a little more.

Geno was so kind and patient with me. Even though he knew I was scared, he quietly waited for me to catch up to him. He was so confident in our love and in us that it was hard to not trust him. Geno stayed for four days and four nights before heading back to Asheville, three and a half hours away. I went back to work. He was going to come back to my house on the following Sunday and stay through Wednesday because I had a business trip scheduled in Chicago the following Thursday. He came back the next Sunday and that night we decided that he would meet me in Chicago and then he was scheduled to meet his friends in Las Vegas the following Monday while I had another business trip scheduled in Houston that same week. Since he was going to meet me in Chicago, he asked me to cancel my trip to Houston and go to Vegas with him, instead. It was in that moment, while sitting on the floor of my TV room talking about my going to Vegas with him, that he said that we should just get married while we were in Vegas! I laughed because it seemed so absurd. I didn't believe that he was serious, so initially

I just disregarded the comment. Still, we were both overjoyed at the prospect of being able to spend so much time together.

By this time, I had told my children – who were all adults – that I had met a wonderful man and that we were going to go to Vegas to visit some friends of his. My oldest daughter, Mona, jokingly told me not to get married while I was there! Geno went back to Asheville on Wednesday and then met me in Chicago the following day. We spent four days in the Windy City before flying to Vegas on Sunday night October 4, 2015.

We arrived in Vegas late on Sunday night. Geno told the hotel clerk who checked us in that we were there to get married and the clerk gave us an upgraded suite. He even gifted us with a bottle of champagne! When we walked into the room, I could not believe how magnificent it was! It had a full kitchen, living room, bedroom, and amazing bathroom. We had a corner room at the Vdara Hotel, with a view of the beautiful water feature that played each and every night. I remember feeling like I was living in a dream. Here I was in this amazingly vibrant, alive city with a man I had only met a few short days before and I was more at peace and in love than I had ever been in my entire life. I remember that Geno fell asleep very quickly that night and I took a little bit longer. In the darkness, all I felt was love, just complete and utter love for this man. In many ways, I had been expecting him to show up and in other ways I worried that he would never find me. This is how my mind works – it quickly swings from one extreme to the other. The next morning, I was awakened by Geno, asking me if I still wanted to get married. "Sure, I guess," I said, and then I went back to sleep. I woke up, again, a couple of hours later, and Geno had everything planned out. He was ready to implement the "Getting Married in Vegas Plan"! I fell into line with the plan only because I thought, *How, can this possibly all come together?* When we got into the cab and gave our driver the address, he asked "Isn't this where you go to get a marriage license?" We both looked at each other and nodded, "Yes!" As he drove us there, he asked if we had a place picked out to get married in and we told him that we had not yet gotten that far in our "Getting Married in Vegas Plan." Our cab driver, Chris, who was a retired dentist that now owned his own cab service in Vegas, became our wedding planner. He even waited with us at the wedding chapel and then took us back to the hotel afterwards, as a married couple!

I quickly learned to never underestimate Geno Delaini when he sets his mind to something. Somehow, despite not having completed the online application for the marriage license, not having a place picked out to have the ceremony and even with a torrential downpour in between, we were married just after 12:00 PM! Even now, looking back, I'm shocked at how it all came together. Geno would say that during our marriage ceremony when the minister asked me to say my wedding vows, I looked completely frozen. Which was, of course, true. Geno and I had requested the drive-through wedding package at the "Little White Chapel." When we went inside to pay for our wedding, the officiant that oversees the weddings at the chapel had a trainee with him and he asked us if we would be willing to walk down the aisle of the chapel and allow his trainee to conduct his last wedding ceremony so that he could be officially certified. This would allow the trainee officiant to perform ceremonies on his own. We agreed, but I assumed that this was just a formality and that Geno, and I would still be "officially" married in the taxi that brought us to the chapel by our driver, Chris. Instead, when we got to the end of the aisle of the chapel, the trainee officiant asked us to recite our vowels and when it was my turn I said, "I didn't think this was real?" Apparently, it was real, and Geno was just rolling with the process while I stood frozen in place. It took me a few seconds to settle into the moment, but I did. Geno was holding tightly onto my hands and while I don't remember exactly what I said to him, I do know that it was official! In that moment, my head was spinning with shame as I thought about all the times that I had married for the wrong reasons, and I hoped and prayed that I was not making yet, another, big mistake.

When we got back to the hotel, we immediately sat down to eat lunch in the hotel restaurant. Halfway through our meal, one of the couples that Geno was expecting arrived. After their brief introduction to me, things quickly settled into busy chatter as we waited for the second couple to arrive. All six of us met for dinner that night and the other couples teased Geno and I by encouraging us to get married since we were already in Vegas. They had absolutely no idea that we had already gotten married earlier that same day. Initially, we were unsure about whether or not to share our news with his friends since neither of us had even told any of our children, about our marriage. In that moment, we both decided that we needed time to settle into our new marriage before sharing it with others.

After spending the evening with Geno's long-time friends, we finally made it back to our hotel room as a married couple. It felt like we were in our own little cocoon, with our own secret. I was so in love with this man, and it felt so different than anything that I had ever experienced before. I felt so safe with this man, and I could feel myself trusting him more and more. The more I trusted him, the more my fears and insecurities began to dissipate. When I married Geno, I was 59 years old and I had only ever had alcohol one time in my entire life. Growing up with an alcoholic father taught me to never ever drink alcohol. At the age of 50, I had gone on a Girl's Trip with my C-K girlfriends. One of my friends brought along a bottle of champagne to toast my 50th birthday. Of course, my friends were all anxious for me to finally taste alcohol! On that trip we celebrated with a mimosa cocktail, and I even had a few sips. Fast forward almost 10 years later and Geno poured me some champagne that the hotel manager had gifted to us, and he left it on my bedside table. By the time he walked around the bed and poured his own drink, I had gulped my entire glass of champagne down, just like it was water. I did not know that it is best to not drink alcohol quickly, especially when you are a novice drinker. I immediately felt woozy and laid down flat on the bed. I felt like my head was glued to the bed and I could not sit up for several hours. To this day Geno loves to tell this wedding night story whenever anyone asks me if I would like a drink, which I respectfully decline. To this day, I have never had any more alcohol but it does make for a funny story about how we spent our honeymoon!

The next day we had some plans to go hiking and do some exploring with the other couples. We had a great time, and the other couples, again, kept encouraging us to get married. Geno had been lifelong friends with both of these other couples and they were very supportive of Geno marrying me because he had previously already reported to both couples that he had found "the One." They totally trusted his judgement, and it didn't matter to them how long we had actually known each other. It was nice to feel so supported by all of them.

After a day of hiking and adventure, we met for dinner. We had a delightful time at dinner in our private room at the restaurant, and the other couples welcomed me with open arms. Eventually, I couldn't wait any longer, and when all three of us women left to go the bathroom together, I abruptly blurted out, "Geno and I got married yesterday!" as we made our way to the bathroom. They both stopped in their tracks and squealed with excitement, right in the middle of the restaurant. Then they hugged me with tears in their eyes – they were thrilled for us! They couldn't wait to get back to the private room where we were eating to tell their husbands and to hug Geno! Finally, someone knew our secret besides Geno and I and our taxi driver, Chris.

The rest of the week was magical. We ate, talked, shopped, and did the Vegas thing, up until it was time to depart.

Geno and I were both living in a fantasy world because we had not told either of our families about our marriage. We had agreed to wait until we returned home. Geno would go on to Asheville and tell his children and then make the necessary preparations to move to Durham to live with me. While, I would somehow corral all of my kiddos together and tell them that we had gotten married. I knew that telling my kids about my marriage to Geno would come with mixed emotions. My children had watched me fall in and out of love with several men since my youngest daughter, Kylie, had started high school.

While Geno and I were waiting at the "Little White Chapel" to get married, my phone rang; it was my oldest daughter, Mona. I felt a wave of nervousness and perhaps even a touch of shame. I did not want her to worry and for a moment I questioned my hasty decision to get married to Geno. My head was swirling; I was vacillating between complete bliss and utter shock! She asked me how things were going and we briefly chatted. Before we hung up, she jokingly said again, "Just don't get married, okay?" We both laughed and ended our call. Learning to trust in my own decision was new for me. I looked over at Geno, who was having a conversation with another couple that were also waiting to get married in the "Little White Chapel". I took a deep breath, closed my eyes for a moment and remembered why I was there. I felt at peace about my decision.

My relationship history had been a long and winding road for both me and for my children. They loved me unconditionally but they all recognized how easily I fallen for men who were not, always, deserving of me. This is the history that I had to face when on October 11, 2015, I gathered my children at my oldest daughter's house to tell them the news about Geno and me. Two of my sons were unable to attend so we had them on FaceTime so that I could tell everyone at once. I shared with them my news that Geno and I got married while we were in Vegas the previous week. Everyone was excited for me, except for my youngest daughter, Kylie. I anticipated that she would have the most difficulty and as predicted, her siblings surrounded and supported her to help her navigate through her feelings.

Sharing our commitment with my children; I felt such a relief when it was over. I felt like I had been waiting my whole life to find this man, and now that we finally had each other, I wanted my kids to know that I was happy. My relationships had taken me on a long journey, but they had all led me to this man, at this time in my life! Finally, I had found the person that I was meant to be with for the rest of our lives. I felt blessed. I also understood my children's hesitation and concern when it came to my relationships. I understood that they had been on an emotional rollercoaster with me as their mother. However, I was exactly where I was meant to be. I trusted that eventually my children would see this for themselves, and eventually they did!

I can step back now and clearly see how unprepared I was when I entered adulthood. When a child grows up in an environment where adults are absent and lessons are few and far between, growth is left to life experiences. When life experiences are limited and confined to a small town, the end result is someone who is not prepared for adulthood. When I became a mother at the age of 25, I was still a young girl in the body of an adult woman. I can now look back at that young mother and have compassion for her shortcomings. That being said, my children deserve the very best from me.

There were times, on my journey with my children, that my best, simply wasn't good enough. My children taught me to work hard so that I could, eventually, become the mother that they deserved. I started college at the age of 25 and I finished my fourth and final degree when I was 45 years old. I was pregnant with Karter when I started my college education and by the time I finished my PhD, four degrees later, Karter was 20 years old. The good thing about learning so many life lessons later in life is that I was as anxious to share them with my children as I was to learn them for myself.

My children deserve a parent who is whole, present, and attentive, yet what they received was a flawed individual determined to grow into the parent they truly deserved. Did I succeed? There were moments when I was exactly who they needed, when they needed me. But there were also many times I fell short, and for those instances, I seek their forgiveness. Thankfully, over time, I evolved into the mother my children needed me to be. Although I wasn't as present or aware as I would have liked, my children showed remarkable resilience, allowing me the space to learn the lessons they were trying to impart all along.

Reflecting on my life, I can distinctly identify three phases. The first phase was my childhood, which feels like a missed opportunity to equip a young girl with the essential life skills necessary for her future. Sadly, the next phase of adulthood arrived prematurely, but it was during this time that I discovered mentors, teachers, friends, therapists, and guiding spirits who illuminated my path until I learned to shine on my own.

Now, I find myself in the present—an accomplished wife, mother, grandmother, and dedicated professional with numerous degrees and years of experience in the medical field. I am finally able to love and nurture my family as I always envisioned. If I could return to my younger self, I would gently reassure that scared little girl, whispering, "I am here with you, always."

In this current phase, I also face the reality of being a retiree. It's difficult to feel completely prepared for retirement, and I am still navigating through these uncharted waters. Some days are filled with accomplishments, while others leave me feeling unproductive, unsatisfied, or incomplete. During those moments, I strive to show compassion to the woman I have become, grateful for the myriads of opportunities life has presented me. This precious gift of life has offered experiences I could never have envisioned as a child. I hope my life serves as a testament to the truth and the countless blessings that arise when truth is uncovered. While betrayal has been part of my journey, it does not define my story.

My blessings are abundant, and I greet each day as a chance to learn what it means to be retired. I carry with me the many gifts I have received throughout my journey. The future remains a mystery, but I eagerly anticipate what lies ahead as it unfolds. I am eternally grateful to those who have illuminated my path, and I am now ready to be a guiding light for myself and others on their journeys toward awareness, truth and fulfillment.

EPILOGUE

Letter to My Children

Dear Karter, Mona, Karson, Kaiden and Kylie

I want to thank each of you for your patience with me as I slowly learned what I needed to know about how to be your mom. I can admit that there were some trying times with each of you, but now those experiences, which at the time challenged me, have been overshadowed by the immense love that I have for every one of you. I have been so blessed to be the mother of five amazing children, and there is nothing that I have accomplished in my life that is more precious to me than loving you and helping you grow and thrive.

To Karter, my firstborn, you were the perfect child for such a young and inexperienced mother. You gave me confidence in myself as a mother because it was so effortless to parent such a sweet and kind boy. You were the best big brother that any sibling could ever have.

To Mona, my chosen child, you completed our family at just the right moment. You taught me to believe in myself, and your quiet spiritual awareness has always been a source of comfort for me. You have given each of us so much more than we could have ever imagined. I have been blessed to have you as my daughter.

To Karson, my second son, I have always said that you were born with a light inside you that attracted others to you and which left you without the ability to recognize or navigate boundaries. While this light made you difficult to parent, it has also made you a gift to those who know you. You taught me to understand that while my children may be born of me, they do not belong to me. I was but your blessed caretaker for a brief period in time.

To Kaiden, my third son. Never has a child fought harder to be born and never was a child more wanted than you. You taught me to always believe in miracles. The sheer miracle of your birth and your subsequent life served as a living testament to me to never underestimate the power of God.

To Kylie, my baby. You are the holder of my heart. Never was a pregnancy more of a surprise than you were to me. You reminded me that my job as your mother was to prepare you to leave home so you could make your own way in the world. You were my greatest exercise in faith because I had to let you go of you, before my heart was ready for you to leave.

My advice for each of you is to never allow missteps, misunderstandings or secrets to stay between your relationships with each other. Forever *recognize the unique gift that each of you have been given because of the love that you have for each other. Never take this gift for granted.*

If I could go back in time and give myself one piece of advice, I would tell myself to worry less because in the end all five of my children blossomed into kind, loving, spiritual humans, as well as becoming the best parents to my beautiful grandchildren.

Wishing you much love and light
Mom

www.ingramcontent.com/pod-product-compliance
Lightning Source LLC
Chambersburg PA
CBHW021144160426
43194CB00007B/683